A SEASON IN HELL
AND
ILLUMINATIONS

ARTHUR RIMBAUD

A SEASON IN HELL
AND
ILLUMINATIONS

Translated by
MARK TREHARNE

J. M. Dent London

First published in Great Britain in 1998
by J. M. Dent

Consultant Editor
Tim Mathews

A CIP catalogue record for this book
is available from the British Library.

ISBN 0 460 87958 8

Typeset by SetSystems Ltd, Saffron Walden, Essex
Set in 10½pt Sabon
Printed in Great Britain by Butler & Tanner Ltd, Frome and London

J. M. Dent
Weidenfeld & Nicolson
The Orion Publishing Group Ltd
Orion House
5 Upper Saint Martin's Lane
London, WC2H 9EA

CONTENTS

Note on the Author and Translator vi

Acknowledgements vii

Chronology of Rimbaud's Life and Times viii

Introduction xix

Note on the Text xxxii

A SEASON IN HELL 1

Notes 55

ILLUMINATIONS 57

Notes 157

Some Responses to Rimbaud 159

Suggestions for Further Reading 163

Index of English Titles 165

Index of French Titles 166

NOTE ON THE AUTHOR
AND TRANSLATOR

ARTHUR RIMBAUD was born in 1854 in Charleville
(Ardennes). Highly intelligent and talented, he started to
write at an early age. As an adolescent he increasingly
revolted against authority and developed his precocious talent
with striking independence of spirit. By the age of seventeen
he had written his arguably most famous poem, 'The Drun-
ken Boat', and shortly afterwards he embarked on a turbu-
lent homosexual relationship with the poet Paul Verlaine
which lasted two years and ended with the latter's imprison-
ment after an attempt on Rimbaud's life. The pair lived in
dissipation and poverty, in Paris, Belgium and London, and
the years of their relationship produced some of their most
original work, in particular Rimbaud's *A Season in Hell*
(1873) and *Illuminations* (which was not published until
1886). Rimbaud had rejected writing by the time he was
twenty or so. He spent the later part of his life travelling in
Europe and the Middle East before settling and working in
East Africa, where his career as a trader and gun-runner met
with little financial success. He died in Marseilles in 1891 at
the age of thirty-seven. His collected work was published
posthumously in 1898.

MARK TREHARNE taught in the French Department at the
University of Warwick between 1969 and 1992. He now
works as a translator and has published translations of sev-
eral works by Philippe Jaccottet and of *Les Ruines de Paris*
by Jacques Réda. He is currently working on a translation of
Proust's *Le Côté de Guermantes*.

ACKNOWLEDGEMENTS

I owe a debt to many previous translators of Rimbaud, but particularly to Oliver Bernard (*Arthur Rimbaud: Collected Poems* [Harmondsworth: Penguin, 1962 and 1997]) and to Paul Schmidt (*Arthur Rimbaud: Complete Works* [New York: Harper & Row, 1976]). I want to thank the students who participated in my Rimbaud seminars at Warwick University, my former colleague Brian Rigby, who encouraged me to write about Rimbaud, and Tim Mathews, who first suggested this translation to me. Hilary Laurie of J. M. Dent has been a patient, helpful and cheerful editor: my grateful thanks to her.

More personal thanks must go to Sue Weaver, Ann Sears, Liz Guild and Bruce Lewington for their support and the discussion I have had with them.

My greatest debt is to Simon Gaunt for his unstinting support throughout the whole project: this book is dedicated to him and to the memory of Upali Ekanayake (1938–1971), who first asked me what Rimbaud 'was all about' and responded with a series of paintings.

CHRONOLOGY OF RIMBAUD'S LIFE

Year	Age	Life
1854		Born 20 October in Charleville, Ardennes. His father is an infantry captain, his mother from a family of agricultural proprietors
1860	6	Captain Rimbaud abandons his family for good

CHRONOLOGY OF HIS TIMES

Year	Artistic Context	Historical Events
1854	Dickens, *Hard Times*	Crimean War (1854–6)
1855		Battle of Sebastopol World Fair in Paris
1856		Birth of Imperial Prince in France Birth of Freud
1857	Flaubert, *Madame Bovary* Baudelaire, *Les Fleurs du mal*	Indian Mutiny
1858		Orsini assassination attempt on Napoleon III
1859	Darwin, *On the Origin of Species* Hugo, *La Légende des siècles* (1859–83)	French establish control of Indochina (1859–93) Italian War Beginning of work on the Suez Canal
1860		Beginning of the 'liberal' Empire in France Lincoln becomes President of the United States. French gain Savoie and Nice from Sardinia
1861	Wagner's *Tannhäuser* at Paris Opéra Dickens, *Great Expectations*	Outbreak of American Civil War (1861–5) Beginning of the construction of the Paris Opéra (1861–75)
1862	Flaubert, *Salammbô* Fromentin, *Dominique* Hugo, *Les Misérables* Michelet, *La Sorcière*	Mexican War. World Fair in London. Bismarck becomes Prime Minister of Prussia
1863	Littré dictionary Manet, *Le Déjeuner sur l'herbe* 'Salon des refusés' in Paris	

Year   Age   Life

1865   11   Starts to attend secondary school in Charleville

1869   15   Wins a prize for writing Latin poetry; writes his first
            French poem, 'Les Etrennes des orphelins'

1870   16   May: sends a letter with three poems to the poet Banville
            August–September: runs away from home (to Paris, then
              Douai to the home of his former teacher, Georges
              Izambard, who returns him to Charleville)
            October: second flight from home (to Charleroi, Brussels,
              Douai, where he copies up the poems he has written so
              far). Returned to his mother by the police
1871   17   February: third flight, to Paris by train. He stays there
              about a fortnight and returns home on foot
            [?April–May: putative journey to Paris and participation
              in the Commune: he is soon to write poems in sympathy
              with it]
            May: writes his 'Visionary Letters' ('Lettres du voyant')
            September: after corresponding with Verlaine and sending
              him poems, joins the latter in Paris and frequents the
              same artistic circles. Rimbaud takes with him to Paris his
              most famous poem 'Le Bateau ivre' (The Drunken Boat),
              composed shortly before his departure

Year	Artistic Context	Historical Events
1864	Verne, *Voyage au centre de la Terre* Tolstoy, *War and Peace* (1864–9)	Foundation of Marx's International
1865		Assassination of Lincoln
1866	Dostoevsky, *Crime and Punishment* Verlaine, *Poèmes saturniens*	
1867	Marx, *Das Kapital*, vol. I Death of Baudelaire	World Fair in Paris Liberal reforms in France Canada becomes a Dominion
1868	Dostoevsky, *The Idiot* (1868–9)	Gladstone becomes Prime Minister of Britain
1869	Lautréamont, *Chants de Maldoror* Flaubert, *L'Education sentimentale* Baudelaire, *Le Spleen de Paris* (posthumous) Verlaine, *Les Fêtes galantes*	Opening of Suez Canal
1870	Verne, *Vingt mille lieues sous les mers* Hugo returns from exile to France Death of Dickens	Franco-Prussian War; defeat of Sedan; fall of Napoleon III Siege of Paris (1870–1) Beginning of Third Republic (1870–1940)
1871	Zola, *Les Rougon-Macquart* (1871–93)	Thiers elected President of the Republic. Paris Commune enacts first socialist programme in Europe; brutally suppressed in May Trade unions legalized in Britain

Year   Age   Life

1872   18   January: Rimbaud and Verlaine are by this time leading a
             dissolute life together (alcohol, hashish, opium) in the
             Latin Quarter, and Verlaine starts quarrelling violently
             with his wife
             February–March: Rimbaud returns to Charleville, where
             he composes further poems
             May: returns to Paris. [?Starts writing some of
             Illuminations]
             July: leaves with Verlaine for Belgium
             September: Rimbaud and Verlaine leave for England and
             install themselves in London. They frequent exiled
             Communards. Rimbaud returns home for Christmas

1873   19   Rimbaud back in London: obtains reader's ticket at
             British Museum
             April: leaves for the family farm at Roche and starts
             writing 'the pagan book' that will become *A Season in
             Hell*
             May: returns to London with Verlaine
             July: a further quarrel with Verlaine, who leaves for
             Belgium. Rimbaud joins him there on 7 July and three
             days later Verlaine shoots at him and wounds him.
             Verlaine imprisoned. Rimbaud returns to Roche, finishes
             A Season in Hell in August and has it published in
             Brussels. Returns to Paris in the autumn

1874   20   Returns to London with the poet Germain Nouveau and
             stays in Britain most of the year

1875   21   February–April: in Stuttgart as a private tutor. Last
             meeting with Verlaine in March. [?Gives Verlaine the
             manuscript of *Illuminations*]
             May: on foot to Italy. Stays in Milan. Returns to
             Charleville in the autumn. Studies various languages
             (Italian, Spanish, Arabic). Learns the piano

1876   22   Enlists in the Dutch Colonial Army and travels to Batavia.
             Deserts and returns to France

1877   23   May: in Bremen. June: in Stockholm

1878   24   November: embarks for Alexandria from Genoa.
             December: job as building foreman in Cyprus

Year	Artistic Context	Historical Events
1872	Verlaine, *Romances sans paroles* (1873–4) Nietzsche, *The Birth of Tragedy*	
1873		German troops leave France. MacMahon elected president of the French Republic after resignation of Thiers Death of Napoleon III
1874	First Impressionist exhibition in Paris	Disraeli Prime Minister in Britain
1875	Bizet, *Carmen*	
1876	Mallarmé, *L'Après-midi d'une faune* Twain, *The Adventures of Tom Sawyer*	Creation of French West Africa (1876–98)
1877	Flaubert, *Trois Contes* Degas, *L'Absinthe* Zola, *L'Assommoir*	Legislative elections in France: Republican victory Queen Victoria becomes empress of India
1878		World Fair in Paris

Year   Age   Life

1879   25   Ill with typhoid, returns to France

1880   26   Returns to Cyprus in March and by July is seeking
            employment in the Red Sea ports. Contract in Aden in
            November with a commercial company. Sent to their
            branch in Harar (Abyssinia) in December

1882   28   Aden. His employers ask him to explore the territories of
            Somaliland and Galla

1883   29   Returns to Harar. December: sends a report to the *Société
            de Géographie* on his explorations in the Ogadine
            region. It is published the following year

1884   30   March: forced to leave Harar by political events; returns
            to Aden

1885   31   Decides to try and make his fortune in arms traffic with
            Menelik, king of Choa. His departure is delayed

1886   32   May and June issues of *La Vogue* publish *Illuminations*
            with a preface by Verlaine
            Rimbaud sets out for Choa in October

1887   33   Is cheated by Menelik. The expedition is disastrous

1888   34   Back in Harar he gives up arms traffic. Installs a
            warehouse and sets up a commercial agency. His
            business enterprises are not successful

Year	Artistic Context	Historical Events
1879	Dostoevsky, *The Brothers Karamazov*	Grévy becomes president of the French Republic
1880	Zola, *Nana* Death of Flaubert	First Ferry Ministry Amnesty for the Communards
1881	Flaubert, *Bouvard et Pécuchet* James, *The Portrait of a Lady*	Ministry of Gambetta France establishes a protectorate over Tunisia
1882		Fall from power and death of Gambetta Jules Ferry Laws secularize primary education, making it free and compulsory Crash of the Union Générale bank
1883	Maupassant, *Une Vie*	French occupy Madagascar, which will become a French colony in 1896
1884	Huysmans, *A rebours* Verlaine, *Les Poètes maudits*	Trade unions legalized in France
1885	Maupassant, *Bel-Ami* Zola, *Germinal* Death of Hugo	Grévy re-elected president of France
1886	Stevenson, *Dr Jekyll and Mr Hyde* Last Impressionist exhibition	Gladstone elected Prime Minister in Britain
1887		Failure of Boulanger's *coup d'état* Sadi Carnot elected president of the French Republic Golden Jubilee of Queen Victoria
1888	Maupassant, *Pierre et Jean* Strindberg, *Miss Julie*	William II emperor of Germany
1889		Second International created at the Congress of Paris Eiffel Tower inaugurated at Paris World Fair

Year   Age   Life

1891	37	Suffers from violent pain in the knee and returns to France. Hospitalized in Marseilles, where his right leg is amputated. After a couple of months back with his family in the Ardennes, he is re-admitted to hospital in Marseilles where he dies 10 November
1898		First relatively complete edition of Rimbaud's work published by Mercure de France

Year	Artistic Context	Historical Events
1890	Claudel, *Tête d'or* Huysmans, *Là-bas* Ibsen, *Hedda Gabler* Wilde, *The Picture of Dorian Gray*	Fall of Bismarck
1891	Hardy, *Tess of the d'Urbervilles*	

·

INTRODUCTION

The poet, a magician with insecurity
René Char

Rimbaud's poetic career – all five years or so of it – must be among the most startling in modern literature. In this very short space of time, roughly between the ages of fifteen and twenty, his writing moved rapidly from recognizable Romantic and Parnassian models and accrued increasingly satirical and painful force, conveyed through sarcasm, parody, elements of realism and turns of language not previously exploited in nineteenth-century French poetry to the same degree or effect; he developed a visionary conception of poetry, allegorized in his best-known poem, 'The Drunken Boat',[1] and subsequently embodied and explored in poems that experiment boldly with metrical form, before abandoning prosody altogether for prose writing. *A Season in Hell* and *Illuminations* are his last major poetic works and after them he seems to have repudiated literature unequivocally.

On one side of this creative outburst lies a childhood characterized by the repressively orthodox strictures of a provincial upbringing, administered essentially by a bigoted and close-minded mother (the father, a soldier, had left the family when Rimbaud was six), against which he was to revolt in a series of flights from home and a refusal to return to a school where he had proved himself to be an exceptionally gifted and precocious pupil.

On the other side is a life devoted to restless travelling, a period working in the Middle East and finally in East Africa, where Rimbaud attempted to make a successful career as a trader, during which time he was involved in charting new territory and in gun-running. Forced back to France in 1891 by a cancer in the leg, he died in Marseilles aged thirty-seven.

Between the repressive childhood and the years of travel and trading is a period of stunning creativity. Much of it

centres around the years of Rimbaud's tormented homosexual relationship with the poet Paul Verlaine, who had invited him to Paris and into his life in 1871. The pair lived a vagrant, dissolute life in Paris, Belgium and England before the relationship ended in a shooting drama in Brussels in 1873. Verlaine was imprisoned; Rimbaud emerged relatively unscathed (physically at least) with a bullet in his wrist, and after a short period of hospitalization returned home, completed *A Season in Hell* and had it published in Brussels. He spent 1874 in England, and it is probable that part of *Illuminations* (begun in all likelihood before the composition of *A Season*) was written during this time. He began his travels the following year. His literary career was effectively over.

Rimbaud published little in his lifetime. The only work he did see through to publication was *A Season in Hell*, the book on which he thought his fate depended. But he could not afford to pay the publisher, and the print run remained unearthed until 1901. *Illuminations* was published – most of it at least – in the Symbolist review *La Vogue* in 1886, but not through any instigation of his own. By this time he was of course in Africa, seemingly unaware of any literary reputation or publication and certainly not preoccupied with such matters. The first relatively complete edition of his works was published by Mercure de France in 1898.

It will already be clear, even from this brief résumé, that Rimbaud's career contains enough to feed a myth. And he was indeed extensively mythologized and idolized, particularly by the French Surrealist poets, for whom he represented a figure of revolt against orthodoxy, the seeker of a formula that would equate poetry with action. Literary scholarship has been busy for years de-mythologizing Rimbaud, and in the last twenty years or so there have been impressive attempts to examine the text of his works and to address their idiosyncratic, elliptical rhetoric. There are still gaps and enigmas and it seems likely that there always will be. Much of the power of Rimbaud's writing stems from the ways in which it resists orthodox interpretation and offers a range of provisional readings on which we can endlessly speculate. Speculation may involve further mythology, but it has the advantage of keeping the poetry wonderfully alive.

The two works translated here are powerful and striking, but also very challenging. They are usually accompanied by a plethora of notes which often exceed the length of the texts themselves to the point where exegesis wins the day over the impact of the writing itself. I have deliberately used as little annotation as possible in the hope that the reader will approach the text with openness of mind and with a particular attention to features such as the nature and drift of the syntax, the strangeness of the punctuation, and possibilities of irony and equivocation. These features seem to me to deserve quite as much attention as the emphasis that has long been placed upon 'images' and biographical 'sources' glossed in endless notes. It is, initially at least, less important to ask 'What does this mean?' than to attend to the patterns and processes of textual composition that contribute so importantly to meaning(s). Rimbaud is not easy to read but nor is he unreadable. It has been pertinently and profitably argued that difficulty and obscurity of language are often important and deliberate strategies on the writer's part to slow down consumer-driven response and to invite a closeness of reading, a questioning that the nature of Rimbaud's text in fact welcomes. This said, it is none the less true that both *A Season in Hell* and *Illuminations* are written in idiosyncratic styles, unique in the canons of nineteenth-century French literature, and that both are initially disorientating in that it is not really possible to situate either of them conveniently in a recognized genre. So, what lines of approach are useful?

Given that both texts prelude a repudiation of writing which is likely to stimulate our interest, and that one of them explicitly takes its farewell of a certain kind of poetic practice, one might start with the question: What sort of writing was it, what idea of poetry, that Rimbaud repudiated? The section of *A Season in Hell* that is particularly relevant here is 'Second Delirium: Alchemy of the Word'. It ironically reviews the 'insanity' of a poetic project which itself echoes a number of Rimbaud's own conceptions of poetry as he had presented them two years earlier in two letters of May 1871. These letters provide a useful point of reference.

They are commonly referred to as 'Les Lettres du voyant' ('Letters of the visionary'): one is addressed to a former

school teacher, Izambard, the other to a poet friend, Paul Demeny.[2] The letters are not systematic exposés of a poetic doctrine, but impetuous, sarcastic explosions of enthusiasm and rejection, championing a handful of poets Rimbaud admires and excoriating a whole body of others whose work does not match up to his own ideal of a visionary poetry. That ideal is expressed in a series of excited and assertive statements which have all too often been used as explanations of Rimbaud's poetry rather than as indications of intention. Nor is the sense of many of them self-evident. What the letters make clear is that the poet will deepen and cultivate self-knowledge with the aim of becoming a seer, a vehicle of supreme knowledge, a *voyant* or visionary. Here is nothing that we would not find (perhaps in less extreme form) in a Romantic theory of poetry. Where Rimbaud parts company with the Romantic poet is in his conception of the self. In theory, Romantic lyric invited the reader to assume a stability of self and a unity and responsibility of personal voice which Rimbaud castigates as *egoism*. The famous assertion that '*I* is another' ('JE est un autre') has important implications for the ways we might read his work. What this odd grammatical formulation does is to place the self in an object position and challenge its authority and autonomy, to commit selfhood to complexity. In the letter to Izambard, the idea is glossed thus: 'It is wrong to say, I think. One ought to say I am thought.' And in the Demeny letter: 'I witness my thought as it unfolds: I watch it, listen to it. My bow touches the string: the symphony stirs in the depths, or leaps on to the stage.' The notion that part of thought springs from an unknown source, 'from the depths', introduces elements of the undirected, the irrational into the idea of both self and voice. It seems clear elsewhere in these letters that Rimbaud wanted to cultivate alien and transgressive states of mind (and body) in order to expand knowledge of self-possibility: hence the statement 'The poet makes himself a *visionary* by a long, boundless and systematic *disordering* of *all the senses*.' The word 'systematic' is an important part of this agenda. One needs to bear in mind that the mental and physical phenomena Rimbaud intends to develop can be inspected and understood – ultimately and ideally at least. He

makes it clear that his programme is not an absolute one, that he might not be able to bring it to fruition in his own lifetime and that later poets will continue the work. So despite the often aggressively affirmative nature of his statements in these letters, what we have in effect is more a tentative apprehension of possibilities than an out-and-out conviction. These are the lines of investigation and practice that Rimbaud will explore, not necessarily bring to a conclusion. In terms of a practice of writing, the notions set out in these letters will presumably result in the willingness of the writer to give credit to those elements of consciousness that occur with apparent fortuitousness: the obsessively recurring image or rhythm, an insistent but apparently random formula, in the hope that these phenomena are ultimately susceptible of sense. The important point is that we cannot assume unity of voice in a Rimbaud text and we cannot assume that the writer is 'in his right mind': the speaking subject can be plurivocal, sane, disturbed, and so on.

Rimbaud's arguably best-known poem, 'The Drunken Boat', written like the two 'Voyant' letters in 1871, is an extended metaphor of poetry as an activity that arises from less stable sources than the controlling intellect, the extended and wonder-filled odyssey of a 'boat' set adrift on the ocean of imaginative impulse. Perhaps the most striking feature of this fantastic voyage of the mind and senses is the final homecoming of the desiring self:

> If I desire a European water, it's the pool,
> Cold and dark, where a child, sadly squatting
> In the scent of coming twilight, launches a boat
> As fragile as a butterfly in May.

The shift in scale from the vastness of an imaginative ocean to the child's puddle is a typical figure of Rimbaud's: not merely an ironical return to reality after absorption in the exotic, a reduced sense of ambition that we shall meet with at the end of *A Season in Hell*, but a recognition that the vision of the child – poignantly lost in the past – is an enviable model for the poetic consciousness.

Many of the poetic ambitions voiced in the 'Lettres du voyant' or embodied in poems such as 'The Drunken Boat'

and the notorious sonnet 'Voyelles' ('Vowels'),[3] in which Rimbaud assigns colours to the five vowels, are rejected in 'Second Delirium'. But these are not grounds enough for the claim that *A Season in Hell* is a rejection of literature altogether. One can see why it was once a temptation for critics to read it as Rimbaud's last work, as a repudiation of literary activity, a full stop. Yet the (still disputed) evidence points to the likelihood that *Illuminations* was written both before and after it, so that it is unlikely that we can confidently read *A Season* as a rejection of the kind of writing exemplified by the other work. On the other hand, Rimbaud did not publish *Illuminations* himself and, for all we know to the contrary, he might never have bothered to do so. The question remains open. The final section of *A Season* takes its leave of much more than a literary practice; it announces a different series of concerns, a different kind of perspective.

The 'Second Delirium' segment of the work is none the less very much concerned with the 'insanity' of a certain type of poetic project and reviews it ironically. It ends with the statement 'All that is over' and an ambiguous formulation which in French can mean either 'I know how to greet beauty' or 'I know how to say farewell to beauty' (I have tried to equivocate between these competing senses in the translation). Interestingly, this final line addresses itself to 'beauty' (as opposed, say, to poetry or literature), and it echoes the opening of the whole work, where 'Beauty' is insulted. Here, it would seem, the notion of beauty is relativized, put in its place: it no longer has the absolute value ascribed to it by its capital letter in the opening segment of *A Season*, where we can read it as a synecdoche for the Romantic cult of Beauty; nor does it seem to be associated any longer with the happiness of 'one long banquet of open hearts and flowing wine' (lyrical effusion?) evoked at the very beginning of the work. By the same token, the whole practice of poetry as an 'alchemy of the word' is reviewed and severely judged. It is described as a highly ambitious project: words as potential magic, an alchemy that can transform experience and reach out towards a perfected world: 'every piece of magic you can name – I believed in it ... I flattered myself that I could invent a poetic language that would eventually be accessible

to all the senses ... I noted down things that cannot be expressed.' The striking and enigmatic lyrics that are placed in the text as illustrations of such a practice – and they are among Rimbaud's finest – are presented ironically as somehow inadequate, falling short of what the narrator has to say about his broader experience in the course of *A Season in Hell* as a whole. If Beauty has been demoted, so has lyric poetry.

In a sense, the visionary claims of the 'Voyant' letters and the practice of lyric poetry are, if not entirely repudiated, ironized and distanced in 'Second Delirium' and elsewhere in *A Season*, which is very different from saying that literature has been repudiated. It is also a work devoted to more than a review of visionary claims for poetry. The crisis it records and from which it seems to stem is an existential one involving the protagonist's relation to history and nationality, to politics, labour, love and coupledom, religion and ideology. There is already evidence of some of these concerns in the Demeny letter of 1871, where Rimbaud was anxious to relate the poetic project to a life of action, to political and social life, in all likelihood inspired by the tragically short-lived upsurge of a shared cultural programme in the Paris Commune towards which we know that he was sympathetic, and in which he may have been briefly involved. He certainly frequented exiled Communards in London before writing *A Season*. It is clear too that his admiration for the poetry of Ancient Greece is bound up with the idea of poetry as an integral part of life and action, and one can imagine that he had in mind the way the work of the Greek tragedians was related to the life of the polis. The references to Greek culture in his writing often signal an ideal of democracy and cultural participation. Certainly Rimbaud would like to equate poetry and action, his seer-poet becoming 'responsible for humanity ... a multiplier of progress' or even being endowed with a vision ahead of his time. The poet's relation to such concerns is examined in *A Season* from a passionately angry and highly frustrated standpoint. The anger is directed at any kind of received idea, at unquestioned orthodoxies of all kinds: assumptions about religion (although ironically the work takes its setting from Christian mythology

and much of its terminology as well), the nature of justice, the institution of marriage as a model for human relationships, the possibility of love, the distribution of human labour. Human greed and stupidity are seen to dominate a world vowed to self-seeking ends: childhoods repressed in the interests of bourgeois adulthood and the perpetuation of complacently convenient social mores; the power-driven aims of militant Christianity; or the greed implicit in colonial imperialism instigated and maintained by military violence, deceit and missionary propaganda. Gestures towards charity, altruism, love and fraternity are strangled by an awareness of evil motives. Nothing, it seems to me, is really resolved in this unnerving work. The protagonist finally emerges from his *agon* to make a series of statements that suggest he has put the past behind him, that the crisis is over, but we are not really offered any redeemed picture of this writer's situation in an unaccommodating world. *A Season in Hell* leaves a whole series of agonized cries for help in the mind of its reader, and this, among other things, is a large part of its force. The work could so easily have reverted to a nostalgic brooding on originary myths of wisdom and piety, and it never lets itself do this: its ultimate echoes are howls for ethical imperatives like charity and the 'innocence' of open-mindedness. The poet-protagonist emerges with a diminished and solitary sense of ambition: if the world cannot be transformed, it can be attended to and witnessed in its immediacy ('One needs to live utterly in the present') with the essential responses to hand – 'truth within one soul and one body'.

A Season in Hell has a particularly modernist slant to it in that it exposes and unravels assumptions, not to resolve them but to leave them open-ended, prone to questioning and uncomfortable involvement. To embody anger and frustration so immediately in written form is highly exacting and Céline is the only French author I can think of who rivals Rimbaud in this respect. Interestingly, both writers have a highly idiosyncratic syntax. Rimbaud's odd punctuation is important in this respect: exclamation- and question-marks register important signals to irony and dramatically emotive statement (the work seems to me to cry out for performance), but, more than this, the use of the dash merits special attention: it vari-

ously suggests hesitations, mood-reversal, sudden switches in perspective, pregnant silence, departures into irony, sarcasm, irrational outburst, anguished outcry and the like. It can also have an elliptical function, implying that the thought is running too fast for the words, and suggesting urgency, breathlessness and a desperate need to get everything down on paper. This is not tranquil recollection, but thought and feeling crowding in upon the writer and clamouring for utterance. There is a rapidity in this style that comes near to vertigo.

We can read *A Season in Hell* as an acutely agonized dramatization of the modern poet's situation, of the nature of his/her function in the world, of the function of poetry in what had developed into an industrial and consumer society in nineteenth-century France. It is as if the world of the lyric voice has been submerged, if not quite drowned, by a materialism and a set of nominal orthodoxies that have little or no place for private utterance, let alone visionary orientation and poetry equated with action as an integral part of a culture. The 'splendid cities' of a utopian culture are not for today. The final lines of the work sound solitary and denuded. Much as they strain towards assertion, they also sound like a bid for survival.

The conflicting picture offered in *A Season in Hell* of poetic expression pitting itself against competing discourses such as religion, bourgeois ideologies, commerce and politics, and all but submerged by them, is more implicitly addressed in *Illuminations*. Here Rimbaud adopts a very particular style of writing, difficult to characterize but certainly assimilable to what was known as the prose poem in nineteenth-century France. The central figure in its development is Baudelaire, who introduced his collection of prose poems *Parisian Spleen* as a musical, flexible prose that could adapt itself not only to lyrical impulse but to more irregular impulses of imagination and to the more violent 'jolts of consciousness (and conscience)'. It is a form of writing that Baudelaire particularly associates with the frequentation of urban life, the unnerving perplexities and complex realities of the modern city. Rimbaud admired Baudelaire greatly, but with the reservation

that his world is too 'artistic', as if the writing was ultimately too bound up with aesthetic concern and the cult of the Beauty insulted in *A Season in Hell*. His view – certainly over-simplistic and characteristically peremptory – may have been directed essentially at Baudelaire's verse rather than the prose poetry: it is difficult to know. Whatever the case, it is interesting that both poets feel the need to move away from verse and adopt the prose poem as a 'new form' of discourse closely associated with their respective notions of modernity. Critics have associated the prose poem with a lawless form of writing, not susceptible to convenient genre classification: it can use at will and at once the conventions of narrative discourse, the figures of poetry, or non-literary modes like the slogan, the tourist guide and so on, in a heterogeneous collage that is constantly shifting its linguistic registers and thereby its perspectives. All this suggests a decentred and plurivocal discourse subversive of any convenient assumption a reader might be tempted to make about a piece of writing. Functioning as a strategy of defamiliarization, the prose poem invites a reading that will ideally always start from scratch without predisposition or any support of reliable expectation (such as that conferred very often by a title). 'Inventions of the unknown demand new forms', as Rimbaud put it in 'Les Lettres du voyant'.

The almost complete rejection of verse in *Illuminations* (and significantly its two verse pieces are in *free* verse), and the adoption of the more fragmented registers of the prose poem, offer both a freedom of discourse and tone and also an implicit rejection of the sense of order and harmony conveyed by verse. As part of the language of poetry, the regularity of metrical form makes its own statement about perception of the world and about stability. So does the implied unity of the lyric 'voice' which we have seen disrupted in Rimbaud's notions of the self. To abandon these is to opt for a different perception, and in the case of *Illuminations* the overall optic of the work is variously fragmented, contradictory, decentred, hallucinatory, distorted. At the same time no one would seriously deny that these pieces are poems in the sense that they demand to be read as a process of composition dominated by thinking in images as opposed to

the relatively literal and linear procedure of a more standard prose. The title (and it is not clear whether it is English or French) was glossed by Verlaine as meaning 'coloured plates', which tends to prettify the collection but also points us in the direction of the undoubted visual impact of the work: landscapes, cityscapes, seascapes, clowns and circus folk, interiors, and so on. Yet the more 'visionary' implications of the title are a reminder that the descriptive elements of the work exceed the literal and assume metaphorical significance. It also stresses the figurative senses of light and dark in a collection where the construction of significance runs the whole gamut from vivid impact to downright obscurity.

Illuminations is also a series of mood pictures, but dynamic and strongly unsettled and unsettling ones. It is rarely possible to argue for consistency of mood in a single text, and the implied identity of the voice in and between individual pieces adopts a shifting series of roles, ranging from the lover to the dismayed and disorientated tourist, from the poet to the sales auctioneer, from the ecstatic drug-taker to the soldier shouting orders.

The ultimate impression of this collection is of a kaleidoscope of variously competing elements, tempered by the fact that each piece is titled, and therefore proposes certain expectations of subject or at least an arena of possibilities, though these are often subverted. Figurative language rubs shoulders with quite disparate and more prosaic discourse and genre: the travelogue, the language of administration, of commerce, of the private journal, of prayer and liturgy, of the testamentary legacy, of the army, of narrative fiction. These features of the language function as signals which point us, implicitly or explicitly, towards social and political contexts, towards a materialistic world of consumerism and power which competes aggressively with the lyrical idealism of poetic perceptions. So while there is no hesitation in saying that this is a predominantly poetic work in the sense that it is primarily governed by a proclivity to see the world in terms of images and to give space to fantasy and desire (idyll, utopian vision, mythologized landscape, fable all figure in the collection), it none the less situates the poetic voice in a plurality of competing voices.

Returning to Rimbaud's statement that 'I is another', it is possible to see *Illuminations* as an exemplification of many of its implications. The language of the self is inhabited by a whole diversity of voices stemming from institutionalized sources such as religious and secular systems of education, from adopted orthodoxies and credos, from literature, from popular cliché, and so on almost *ad infinitum*. Those voices can be quite consciously deployed, but they can also be born of unconscious impulse. They can also be directed to literal or figurative ends, to strategies that range from irony to celebration. They can represent harmonious or conflicting systems of meaning and of ethical perspective. In Rimbaud's case the divided, agonistic voice of *A Season in Hell*, pulled in all directions by instabilities of emotion and belief, extends itself in *Illuminations* to embrace the more positive possibilities of a pluralistic notion of the self. It seems to me that Rimbaud's practice of the prose poem represents a liberation from what was previously and more conservatively regarded as poetic voice, and his view of self as a plurality of voices orientates poetry radically towards modernism.

A few further words on the language of the collection. I have already remarked on the idiosyncratic punctuation of *A Season in Hell*, and the same is true of *Illuminations*, probably to a greater extent in that a sentence can often straddle several paragraph divisions. It is also the case that the syntax sometimes promotes ambiguous readings and at times refuses to function grammatically. I take this as deliberate. It is likely too that the reader who is approaching *Illuminations* for the first time will be disconcerted by two further features of the style: the odd use of prepositions which seem to have more of an affective impact than their usual functions as indicators of space and time; and the deictic elements of the text generally, particularly the use of the definite article and demonstratives, but also the correlation of verb tenses, register more than a sense of defamiliarization – they insist on the 'here and now' of the text itself, on what is being constructed in language and how it is being constructed, before we can proceed to examine the question of what the text is trying to represent.[4]

Finally, and this will now be more than apparent, the den-

sity and ambiguities of the two texts in question require more than a single translation, ideally a range of translations to cover the polysemy and the richness of suggestion of the writing. Any translation is an implied act of criticism and selective judgement. What is offered here is a provisional translation and hopefully an invitation to explore further.

References

[1] This can be found in Arthur Rimbaud, *Collected Poems*, translated by Oliver Bernard (London: Penguin, 1997), pp. 165–71. This work is hereafter referred to simply as Bernard.

[2] For the two letters, see Bernard, pp. 5–17. The translations from the letters and other material in the introduction are my own.

[3] Ibid., pp. 171–2.

[4] I have examined these points in more detail in an analysis of one of the *Illuminations*: 'Unstable objects: *acropole* and *barbarie* in Rimbaud's "Villes I"', in Brian Rigby (ed.), *French Literature, Thought and Culture in the Nineteenth Century: A Material World* (London: Macmillan, 1993), pp. 169–83.

NOTE ON THE TEXT

The French text of *A Season in Hell* follows the original edition (Brussels: Alliance Typographique; Poot et Cie, 1873). The text of *Illuminations* is taken from Arthur Rimbaud, *Oeuvres III: Illuminations*, edited by Jean-Luc Steinmetz (Flammarion, 1989). I am grateful to Les Editions Flammarion for permission to reproduce this text. Steinmetz has taken account of recent scholarship and based his text on a reading of the available manuscripts. The reader interested in a facsimile of the manuscripts can consult Claude Jeancolas, *Rimbaud: L'Œuvre intégrale manuscrite* (Paris: Les Éditions Textuel, 1996).

A SEASON IN HELL

«Jadis, si je me souviens bien, ma vie était un festin où s'ouvraient tous les cœurs, où tous les vins coulaient.

Un soir, j'ai assis la Beauté sur mes genoux. – Et je l'ai trouvée amère. – Et je l'ai injuriée.

Je me suis armé contre la justice.

Je me suis enfui. Ô sorcières, ô misère, ô haine, c'est à vous que mon trésor a été confié!

Je parvins à faire s'évanouir dans mon esprit toute l'espérance humaine. Sur toute joie pour l'étrangler j'ai fait le bond sourd de la bête féroce.

J'ai appelé les bourreaux pour, en périssant, mordre la crosse de leurs fusils. J'ai appelé les fléaux, pour m'étouffer avec le sable, le sang. Le malheur a été mon dieu. Je me suis allongé dans la boue. Je me suis séché à l'air du crime. Et j'ai joué de bons tours à la folie.

Et le printemps m'a apporté l'affreux rire de l'idiot.

Or, tout dernièrement m'étant trouvé sur le point de faire le dernier *couac*! j'ai songé à rechercher la clef du festin ancien, où je reprendrais peut-être appétit.

La charité est cette clef. – Cette inspiration prouve que j'ai rêvé!

«Tu resteras hyéne, etc . . .,» se récrie le démon qui me couronna de si aimables pavots. «Gagne la mort avec tous tes appétits, et ton égoïsme et tous les péchés capitaux.»

Ah! j'en ai trop pris: – Mais, cher Satan, je vous en conjure, une prunelle moins irritée! et en attendant les quelques petites lâchetés en retard, vous qui aimez dans l'écrivain l'absence des facultés descriptives ou instructives, je vous détache ces quelques hideux feuillets de mon carnet de damné.

'Long ago, if I remember rightly, my life was one long banquet of open hearts and flowing wine.

One evening, I sat Beauty on my knees. – And I found her bitter. – And I insulted her.

I armed myself against justice.

I fled. You witches, poverty, hatred, my treasure was entrusted to you!

I managed to make all human hope vanish from my mind. To strangle every form of joy, I pounced on it, stealthily, like a wild beast.

I called the executioners so that I could bite the butts of their guns as I died. I have called up plagues, to suffocate myself with sand, with blood. Disaster has been my god. I have lain in the mud. I have dried myself in the crime-infested air. And I've played some fine tricks on madness.

And spring has brought me the hideous laughter of an idiot.

Now quite recently, when I found myself on the point of croaking my last, I thought of looking for the key to the former banquet. Perhaps I would recover my appetite for it.

This key is charity. – A piece of inspiration which proves I have been dreaming!

'You will never stop being a hyena, etc . . .' yells the demon who once wreathed such lovely poppies around my head. 'Go to greet death with all your appetites, with your selfishness and all the deadly sins.'

Ah! there have been too many of them: – But I beg you, my dear Satan, don't look so annoyed! and while we are waiting for the few more little low deeds to complete the quota, and since you appreciate the absence of any descriptive or instructive powers in a writer, here are a few hideous pages torn from my journal of damnation.

MAUVAIS SANG

J'ai de mes ancêtres gaulois l'œil bleu blanc, la cervelle étroite, et la maladresse dans la lutte. Je trouve mon habillement aussi barbare que le leur. Mais je ne beurre pas ma chevelure.

Les Gaulois étaient les écorcheurs de bêtes, les brûleurs d'herbes les plus ineptes de leur temps.

D'eux, j'ai: l'idolâtrie et l'amour du sacrilège; – oh! tous les vices, colère, luxure, – magnifique, la luxure; – surtout mensonge et paresse.

J'ai horreur de tous les métiers. Maîtres et ouvriers, tous paysans, ignobles. La main à plume vaut la main à charrue. – Quel siècle à mains! – Je n'aurai jamais ma main. Après, la domesticité mène trop loin. L'honnêteté de la mendicité me navre. Les criminels dégoûtent comme des châtrés: moi, je suis intact, et ça m'est égal.

Mais! qui a fait ma langue perfide tellement, qu'elle ait guidé et sauvegardé jusqu'ici ma paresse? Sans me servir pour vivre même de mon corps, et plus oisif que le crapaud, j'ai vécu partout. Pas une famille d'Europe que je ne connaisse. – J'entends des familles comme la mienne, qui tiennent tout de la déclaration des Droits de l'Homme. – J'ai connu chaque fils de famille!

———

Si j'avais des antécédents à un point quelconque de l'histoire de France!

Mais non, rien.

Il m'est bien évident que j'ai toujours été race inférieure. Je ne puis comprendre la révolte. Ma race ne se souleva jamais que pour piller: tels les loups à la bête qu'ils n'ont pas tuée.

Je me rappelle l'histoire de la France fille aînée de l'Église. J'aurais fait, manant, le voyage de terre sainte; j'ai dans la tête des routes dans les plaines souabes, des vues de Byzance, des remparts de Solyme; le culte de Marie, l'attendrissement sur le crucifié s'éveillent en moi parmi mille féeries profanes. – Je suis

BAD BLOOD

From my ancestors the Gauls I inherit pale blue eyes, a narrow skull and a lack of skill in fighting. My clothes seem to me to be as barbaric as theirs were. But I don't use butter on my hair.

The Gauls were the clumsiest flayers of beasts and burners of grass of their time.

From them I inherit: idolatry and love of sacrilege; – oh! all the vices, anger, lechery, – wonderful thing, lechery; – and above all lying and laziness.

I loathe all trades. Foremen and workmen, peasants the lot of them, debased. The hand that wields the pen is as good as the hand steering the plough. – What a century of hands! – I shall never get my hand in. And then, servitude goes too far. The decency of begging distresses me. Criminals are as disgusting as men without balls: I've got mine and it's all the same to me.

But! who has given me such a treacherous tongue that, up to now, it has guided and protected my idleness? Without using even my body to make a living, lazier than a toad, I have lived everywhere. There's not a family in Europe I don't know. – I mean families like mine, who owe everything to the Declaration of the Rights of Man.[1] – I've known every young man of good family there is to know!

———

If only I had antecedents at some point or other in the history of France!

But no, nothing.

It is obvious to me that I have always belonged to an inferior race. I don't understand rebellion. My race never rose up except to plunder: like wolves devouring the animal they did not kill.

I remember the history of France, the eldest daughter of the Church. I, a serf, would have made the journey to the Holy Land: my head is full of the routes through the Swabian plains, views of Byzantium, the ramparts of Solyma;[2] the cult of the Virgin, compassion for the crucified one, stir in my mind along with a thousand profane enchantments. – I sit, stricken with leprosy, on

assis, lépreux, sur les pots cassés et les orties, au pied d'un mur rongé par le soleil. – Plus tard, reître, j'aurais bivaqué sous les nuits d'Allemagne.

Ah! encore: je danse le sabbat dans une rouge clairière, avec des vieilles et des enfants.

Je ne me souviens pas plus loin que cette terre-ci et le christianisme. Je n'en finirais pas de me revoir dans ce passé. Mais toujours seul; sans famille; même, quelle langue parlais-je? Je ne me vois jamais dans les conseils du Christ; ni dans les conseils des Seigneurs, – représentants du Christ.

Qu'étais-je au siècle dernier: je ne me retrouve qu'aujourd'hui. Plus de vagabonds, plus de guerres vagues. La race inférieure a tout couvert – le peuple, comme on dit, la raison; la nation et la science.

Oh! la science! On a tout repris. Pour le corps et pour l'âme, – le viatique, – on a la médecine et la philosophie, – les remèdes de bonnes femmes et les chansons populaires arrangés. Et les divertissements des princes et les jeux qu'ils interdisaient! Géographie, cosmographie, mécanique, chimie!...

La science, la nouvelle noblesse! Le progrès. Le monde marche! Pourquoi ne tournerait-il pas?

C'est la vision des nombres. Nous allons à l'*Esprit*. C'est très-certain, c'est oracle, ce que je dis. Je comprends, et ne sachant m'expliquer sans paroles païennes, je voudrais me taire.

————

Le sang païen revient! L'Esprit est proche, pourquoi Christ ne m'aide-t-il pas, en donnant à mon âme noblesse et liberté. Hélas! l'Evangile a passé! l'Évangile! l'Évangile.

J'attends Dieu avec gourmandise. Je suis de race inférieure de toute éternité.

Me voici sur la plage armoricaine. Que les villes s'allument dans le soir. Ma journée est faite; je quitte l'Europe. L'air marin brûlera mes poumons; les climats perdus me tanneront. Nager, broyer l'herbe, chasser, fumer surtout; boire des liqueurs fortes comme du métal bouillant, – comme faisaient ces chers ancêtres autour des feux.

Je reviendrai, avec des membres de fer, la peau sombre, l'œil furieux: sur mon masque, on me jugera d'une race forte. J'aurai

broken pots and nettles at the foot of a wall gnawed away by sunlight. – At some later stage, as a wandering mercenary, I would have bivouacked under the night skies in Germany.

Ah! one thing more: I am dancing at a witches' sabbath in a red clearing, with old hags and children.

I can remember nothing beyond this land and Christianity. I shall never stop seeing myself back in this past. But always solitary; without a family; what language in fact did I speak? I never see myself as a follower of Christ; nor as a follower of the Nobles who were Christ's representatives.

What was I in the last century? I can only see myself as I am today. The wanderers, the vague wars are gone. The inferior race has spread everywhere – the people, as they put it, reason; the nation, science.

Ah! science! Everything has been revised. For the body and the soul, – the viaticum, – we have medicine and philosophy, – old wives' remedies and arrangements of popular songs. As for royal entertainments and the games that kings forbade! we have geography, cosmography, mechanics, chemistry! . . .

Science, the modern idea of nobility! Progress. The world marches forward! Perhaps it will go round in circles too!

It is the vision of numbers. We are moving towards the *Spirit*. What I am saying is absolutely true, the voice of the oracle. I understand, and because I can only express myself in a pagan language, I would rather say nothing.

––––––

Pagan blood returns! The Spirit is at hand, why does Christ not come to my aid and give nobility and freedom to my soul. Alas! the Gospel belongs to the past! the Gospel! the Gospel.

I am starving for God. I have belonged to an inferior race since time began.

And now, here I am on the shores of Brittany. Let the cities light up in the evening. My day is done; I am leaving Europe. Sea air will scorch my lungs: remote climates will tan my skin. To swim, to tramp down grass, to hunt, and above all to smoke; to drink liquor as strong as molten metal – as my beloved ancestors did around their fires.

I shall return, with limbs of iron, a dark skin, and angry eyes: from my mask, people will think I belong to a strong race. I

de l'or: je serai oisif et brutal. Les femmes soignent ces féroces infirmes retour des pays chauds. Je serai mêlé aux affaires politiques. Sauvé.

Maintenant je suis maudit, j'ai horreur de la patrie. Le meilleur, c'est un sommeil bien ivre, sur la grève.

———

On ne part pas. – Reprenons les chemins d'ici, chargé de mon vice, le vice qui a poussé ses racines de souffrance à mon côté, dès l'âge de raison – qui monte au ciel, me bat, me renverse, me traîne.

La dernière innocence et la dernière timidité. C'est dit. Ne pas porter au monde mes dégoûts et mes trahisons.

Allons! La marche, le fardeau, le désert, l'ennui et la colère.

A qui me louer? Quelle bête faut-il adorer? Quelle sainte image attaque-t-on? Quels cœurs briserai-je? Quel mensonge dois-je tenir? – Dans quel sang marcher?

Plutôt, se garder de la justice. – La vie dure, l'abrutissement simple, – soulever, le poing desséché, le couvercle du cercueil, s'asseoir, s'étouffer. Ainsi point de vieillesse, ni de dangers: la terreur n'est pas française.

– Ah! je suis tellement délaissé que j'offre à n'importe quelle divine image des élans vers la perfection.

Ô mon abnégation, ô ma charité merveilleuse! ici-bas, pourtant!

De profondis Domine, suis-je bête!

———

Encore tout enfant, j'admirais le forçat intraitable sur qui se referme toujours le bagne; je visitais les auberges et les garnis qu'il aurait sacrés par son séjour; je voyais *avec son idée* le ciel bleu et le travail fleuri de la campagne; je flairais sa fatalité dans les villes. Il avait plus de force qu'un saint, plus de bon sens qu'un voyageur – et lui, lui seul! pour témoin de sa gloire et de sa raison.

Sur les routes, par des nuits d'hiver, sans gîte, sans habits, sans pain, une voix étreignait mon cœur gelé: «Faiblesse ou force: te voilà, c'est la force. Tu ne sais ni où tu vas ni pourquoi

shall have gold: I shall be idle and brutal. Women nurse such
ferocious invalids on their return from the tropics. I shall be
involved in politics. Saved.

But for now I am damned, I loathe my native land. I'd best
fall into an utterly drunken sleep, by the sea-shore.

————

No one gets away. – I'll take to the roads of this country
again, burdened with my vice, the vice that has driven painful
roots into my side, ever since I grew up . . . it rises to the sky,
beats me, knocks me down, drags me along.

The last trace of innocence and the last shred of diffidence.
I've said it. Not to carry my loathings and my treacheries into
the world.

Come on! Marching, carrying heavy loads, the desert, bore-
dom and anger.

Hire myself to whom? What beast is there to be worshipped?
What holy image to be knocked down? Whose hearts shall I
break? What lies to maintain? – In what blood shall I wade?

Better to be wary of the law. – A hard life, utter mindless
exhaustion, – then to lift the coffin lid with a shrivelled fist, to
sit inside, to suffocate. And thus, no old age, no dangers risked:
terror is not a French emotion.

– God! I am so bereft that I could offer up my urges to
perfection to any divine image you care to name.

My self-denial! My marvellous charity! and I'm still down
here on earth!

De profundis Domine,³ what a fool I am!

————

Even as a small child, I used to admire the hardened convict
who will always return to prison; I visited the bars and rented
rooms he might have consecrated by his presence; I saw the blue
sky and the flowering activity of the countryside *through his
eyes*; I sniffed out his fate on city streets. He had more strength
than a saint, more sense about him than any traveller – and he,
he alone! was witness to his fame and his justification.

On the roads, on winter nights, without shelter, without
clothes, without food, a voice would clutch at my frozen heart:
'Weakness or strength: take a look at yourself, there's strength

tu vas, entre partout, réponds à tout. On ne te tuera pas plus que si tu étais cadavre.» Au matin j'avais le regard si perdu et la contenance si morte, que ceux que j'ai rencontrés *ne m'ont peut-être pas vu.*

Dans les villes la boue m'apparaissait soudainement rouge et noire, comme une glace quand la lampe circule dans la chambre voisine, comme un trésor dans la forêt! Bonne chance, criais-je, et je voyais une mer de flammes et de fumée au ciel; et, à gauche, à droite, toutes les richesses flambant comme un milliard de tonnerres.

Mais l'orgie et la camaraderie des femmes m'étaient interdites. Pas même un compagnon. Je me voyais devant une foule exaspérée, en face du peloton d'exécution, pleurant du malheur qu'ils n'aient pu comprendre, et pardonnant! – Comme Jeanne d'Arc! – «Prêtres, professeurs, maîtres, vous vous trompez en me livrant à la justice. Je n'ai jamais été de ce peuple-ci; je n'ai jamais été chrétien; je suis de la race qui chantait dans le supplice; je ne comprends pas les lois; je n'ai pas le sens moral, je suis une brute: vous vous trompez . . .»

Oui, j'ai les yeux fermés à votre lumière. Je suis une bête, un nègre. Mais je puis être sauvé. Vous êtes de faux nègres, vous maniaques, féroces, avares. Marchand, tu es nègre; magistrat, tu es nègre; général, tu es nègre; empereur, vieille démangeaison, tu es nègre: tu as bu d'une liqueur non taxée, de la fabrique de Satan. – Ce peuple est inspiré par la fièvre et le cancer. Infirmes et vieillards sont tellement respectables qu'ils demandent à être bouillis. – Le plus malin est de quitter ce continent, où la folie rôde pour pourvoir d'otages ces misérables. J'entre au vrai royaume des enfants de Cham.

Connais-je encore la nature? me connais-je? – *Plus de mots.* J'ensevelis les morts dans mon ventre. Cris, tambour, danse, danse, danse, danse! Je ne vois même pas l'heure où, les blancs débarquant, je tomberai au néant.

Faim, soif, cris, danse, danse, danse, danse!

———

Les blancs débarquent. Le canon! Il faut se soumettre au baptême, s'habiller, travailler.

J'ai reçu au cœur le coup de la grâce. Ah! je ne l'avais pas prévu!

in you. You don't know where you are going or why, go everywhere, respond to everything. You've no more risk of being killed than a corpse has.' In the morning my gaze was so vacant and my expression so dead that the people I encountered *possibly didn't even see me.*

In the cities, the mud suddenly seemed red and black, like a mirror when a lamp moves around in the adjoining room, like treasure in the forest! Good luck, I would shout, and I would see an ocean of flames and smoke in the sky; and to left and right, every kind of wealth bursting into flame like a billion thunderbolts.

But orgies and easy relations with women were forbidden me. Not even a companion. I saw myself in front of an angry mob, facing a firing squad, weeping with misery that they would not have been able to understand, and forgiving them! – Like Joan of Arc! – 'Priests, teachers, masters, you are wrong to deliver me up to justice. I have never belonged here with you; I have never been a Christian; I belong to a race which sang on the scaffold; I do not understand the laws; I have no moral sense, I am an animal: you are making a mistake . . .'

Yes, my eyes are blind to your light. I am an animal, a nigger. But I can be saved. You are niggers in disguise, the lot of you, maniacs, savages, misers. Mr shopkeeper, you're a nigger; Mr judge, you too; general, you're a nigger; emperor, you old ratbag, you're a nigger: you've drunk untaxed liquor, satanic brew. – This nation is breathing in fever and cancer. The sick and the old are so law-abiding that they *ask* to be boiled. – The shrewdest thing to do is to leave this continent where madness prowls, seeking hostages for these pitiful people. I am entering the true kingdom of the children of Ham.[4]

Have I reached an understanding of nature? do I know myself? – *Enough words.* I bury the dead in my stomach, Shouts, drums, dance, dance, dance, dance! I can't even imagine the time when the white men disembark, and I shall sink into nothingness.

Hunger, thirst, shouts, dance, dance, dance, dance!

———

The white men are landing. Cannon fire! Now we shall have to submit to being baptized, wearing clothes, working.

My heart has received the deadly blow of saving grace. Ah! I had not foreseen this!

Je n'ai point fait le mal. Les jours vont m'être légers, le repentir me sera épargné. Je n'aurai pas eu les tourments de l'âme presque morte au bien, où remonte la lumière sévère comme les cierges funéraires. Le sort du fils de famille, cercueil prématuré couvert de limpides larmes. Sans doute la débauche est bête, le vice est bête; il faut jeter la pourriture à l'écart. Mais l'horloge ne sera pas arrivée à ne plus sonner que l'heure de la pure douleur! Vais-je être enlevé comme un enfant, pour jouer au paradis dans l'oubli de tout le malheur!

Vite! est-il d'autres vies? – Le sommeil dans la richesse est impossible. La richesse a toujours été bien public. L'amour divin seul octroie les clefs de la science. Je vois que la nature n'est qu'un spectacle de bonté. Adieu chimères, idéals, erreurs.

Le chant raisonnable des anges s'élève du navire sauveur: c'est l'amour divin. – Deux amours! je puis mourir de l'amour terrestre, mourir de dévouement. J'ai laissé des âmes dont la peine s'accroîtra de mon départ! Vous me choisissez parmi les naufragés; ceux qui restent sont-ils pas mes amis?

Sauvez-les!

La raison m'est née. Le monde est bon. Je bénirai la vie. J'aimerai mes frères. Ce ne sont plus des promesses d'enfance. Ni l'espoir d'échapper à la vieillesse et à la mort. Dieu fait ma force, et je loue Dieu.

———

L'ennui n'est plus mon amour. Les rages, les débauches, la folie, dont je sais tous les élans et les désastres, – tout mon fardeau est déposé. Apprécions sans vertige l'étendue de mon innocence.

Je ne serais plus capable de demander le réconfort d'une bastonnade. Je ne me crois pas embarqué pour une noce avec Jésus-Christ pour beau-père.

Je ne suis pas prisonnier de ma raison. J'ai dit: Dieu. Je veux la liberté dans le salut: comment la poursuivre? Les goûts frivoles m'ont quitté. Plus besoin de dévouement ni d'amour divin. Je ne regrette pas le siècle des cœurs sensibles. Chacun a sa raison, mépris et charité: je retiens ma place au sommet de cette angélique échelle de bon sens.

Quant au bonheur établi, domestique ou non ... non, je ne

I have done nothing evil. My days are going to be easy, I shall be spared repentance. I shall not have had the torments of the soul that is almost dead to goodness, with stark light rising like funeral candles. The fate of the son of good family, a premature coffin covered with limpid tears. Undoubtedly debauchery is stupid, vice is stupid; corruption needs to be cast aside. But the clock cannot have reached the point where it only strikes the hour of utter pain! Am I about to be carried off like a child, to play in paradise oblivious of all misfortune!

Quick! are there other lives? – To be wealthy and to sleep soundly is an impossibility. Wealth has always been public property. Divine love alone can confer the keys of knowledge. I can see that nature is only a spectacle of goodness. Farewell to chimeras, to ideals, to error.

The sane song of angels rises from the rescue ship: it is divine love. – Two loves! I can die of earthly love, I can die of devotion. I have left behind souls whose pain will grow because of my departure! You are choosing me from among the shipwrecked; aren't those who remain my friends?

Save them!

Reason is born within me. The world is good. I shall bless life. I shall love my brothers. These are no longer childhood promises. Nor are they the hope of escaping old age and death. God is my strength, and I praise God.

———

I am no longer in love with apathy. Anger, debauchery, madness, whose excitements and disasters I know to the full, – I have laid down the whole of my burden. It is time to weigh up the extent of my innocence without losing our heads.

I would no longer be able to ask for the comfort of a beating. I don't see myself set for a wedding celebration with Jesus Christ for my father-in-law.

I am not a prisoner of my own reason. I have said: God. I need freedom in salvation: how do I set about finding it? I have no more frivolous inclinations. No need now of devotion or divine love. I do not look back with longing on the century of emotion and sensibility. Contempt and charity are both right in their own way: I keep my place at the top of this angelic ladder of common sense.

As for established happiness, domestic or otherwise ... no,

peux pas. Je suis trop dissipé, trop faible. La vie fleurit par le travail, vieille vérité: moi, ma vie n'est pas assez pesante, elle s'envole et flotte loin au-dessus de l'action, ce cher point du monde.

Comme je deviens vieille fille, à manquer du courage d'aimer la mort!

Si Dieu m'accordait le calme céleste, aérien, la prière, – comme les anciens saints. – Les saints! des forts! les anachorètes, des artistes comme il n'en faut plus!

Farce continuelle! Mon innocence me ferait pleurer. La vie est la farce à mener par tous.

———

Assez! Voici la punition. – *En marche!*

Ah! les poumons brûlent, les tempes grondent! la nuit roule dans mes yeux, par ce soleil! le cœur . . . les membres . . .

Où va-t-on? au combat? Je suis faible! les autres avancent. Les outils, les armes . . . le temps! . . .

Feu! feu sur moi! Là! ou je me rends. – Lâches! – Je me tue! Je me jette aux pieds des chevaux!

Ah! . . .

– Je m'y habituerai.

Ce serait la vie française, le sentier de l'honneur!

it's not for me. I am too dissipated, too weak. Work makes life blossom, an old truth: my own life is not grounded enough, it flies off and hovers far above action, that focus of the world's affection.

What an old maid I'm turning into, with my lack of courage to embrace death!

Were God to grant me celestial, ethereal calm, and prayer, – like the old saints. – The saints! strong men! anchorites and artists of whom we have no need now!

Is there no end to this farce! My innocence is enough to make me weep. Life is a farce to be played out by us all.

———

Enough! Here is the punishment. – *Forward march!*

Ah! my lungs are burning, my head is throbbing! darkness surges in my eyes beneath this glaring sunlight! My heart . . . my arms and legs . . .

Where are we going? to battle? I am weak! the others are advancing. Tools, weapons . . . time! . . .

Fire! fire at me! Here! or I'll surrender. – Cowards! – I shall kill myself! throw myself under the horses' hooves!

Ah! . . .

– I shall get used to it.

That would be the French way of life, the path of honour!

NUIT DE L'ENFER

J'ai avalé une fameuse gorgée de poison. – Trois fois béni soit le conseil qui m'est arrivé! – Les entrailles me brûlent. La violence du venin tord mes membres, me rend difforme, me terrasse. Je meurs de soif, j'étouffe, je ne puis crier. C'est l'enfer, l'éternelle peine! Voyez comme le feu se relève! Je brûle comme il faut. Va, démon!

J'avais entrevu la conversion au bien et au bonheur, le salut. Puis-je décrire la vision, l'air de l'enfer ne souffre pas les hymnes! C'était des millions de créatures charmantes, un suave concert spirituel, la force et la paix, les nobles ambitions, que sais-je?

Les nobles ambitions!

Et c'est encore la vie! – Si la damnation est éternelle! Un homme qui veut se mutiler est bien damné, n'est-ce pas? Je me crois en enfer, donc j'y suis. C'est l'exécution du catéchisme. Je suis esclave de mon baptême. Parents, vous avez fait mon malheur et vous avez fait le vôtre. Pauvre innocent! – L'enfer ne peut attaquer les païens. – C'est la vie encore! Plus tard, les délices de la damnation seront plus profondes. Un crime, vite, que je tombe au néant, de par la loi humaine.

Tais-toi, mais tais-toi! ... C'est la honte, le reproche, ici: Satan qui dit que le feu est ignoble, que ma colère est affreusement sotte. – Assez! ... Des erreurs qu'on me souffle, magies, parfums faux, musiques puériles. – Et dire que je tiens la vérité, que je vois la justice: j'ai un jugement sain et arrêté, je suis prêt pour la perfection ... Orgueil. – La peau de ma tête se dessèche. Pitié! Seigneur, j'ai peur. J'ai soif, si soif! Ah! l'enfance, l'herbe, la pluie, le lac sur les pierres, *le clair de lune quand le clocher sonnait douze* ... le diable est au clocher, à cette heure. Marie! Sainte-Vierge! ... – Horreur de ma bêtise.

Là-bas, ne sont-ce pas des âmes honnêtes, qui me veulent du bien ... Venez ... J'ai un oreiller sur la bouche, elles ne m'entendent pas, ce sont des fantômes. Puis, jamais personne ne

NIGHT IN HELL

I've gulped down a whole mouthful of poison. – Thrice blessed be the advice that came my way! – My stomach is on fire. The power of the poison is racking my arms and legs, making me deformed, throwing me to the ground. I am dying of thirst, choking, incapable of crying out. This is hell, eternal torment! See how the flames rise higher! I am burning just as we're told we will. So there! demon!

I once had a glimpse of being converted to goodness and happiness, salvation. Can I describe what I saw? the atmosphere of hell is no place for hymns! There were millions of lovely creatures, a mellow spiritual harmony, strength and peace, noble aspiration, and I don't know what else.

Noble aspiration!

And I am still alive here! – What if damnation is eternal? A man who wants to mutilate himself *is* damned, isn't he? I think I am in hell, therefore I am. That's the catechism at work. I am the slave of my baptism. You, my parents, have brought about my misfortune and created your own. Poor innocent! – Hell cannot touch the heathen. – I am still alive! In a while, the delights of damnation will intensify. Quick, give me a crime to commit and let me fall into extinction, judged by human law.

Shut up, oh shut up! ... Everything is shame and reproach in this place: Satan telling me that I am not worthy of hellfire, that my anger is utterly stupid. – Enough! ... Lies whispered to me, magic spells, unreal perfumes, puerile music. – And to think that I possess the truth, that I have a vision of justice: my judgement is sound and certain, I am ready for perfection ... Pride. – The skin on my head is drying up. Have mercy! Lord, I am afraid. And thirsty, so thirsty! Ah! childhood, the grass, the rain, the lake water over the stones, *the moonlight when the church clock struck twelve* ... the devil is in the clock tower, at this very moment. Mary! Holy Virgin! ... – The horror of my stupidity.

Are those not honourable souls over there, wishing me well ... Come ... there is a pillow gagging me, they cannot hear me, they are ghosts. Besides, no one ever gives a thought to

pense à autrui. Qu'on n'approche pas. Je sens le roussi, c'est certain.

Les hallucinations sont innombrables. C'est bien ce que j'ai toujours eu: plus de foi en l'histoire, l'oubli des principes. Je m'en tairai: poëtes et visionnaires seraient jaloux. Je suis mille fois le plus riche, soyons avare comme la mer.

Ah ça! l'horloge de la vie s'est arrêtée tout à l'heure. Je ne suis plus au monde. – La théologie est sérieuse, l'enfer est certainement *en bas* – et le ciel en haut. – Extase, cauchemar, sommeil dans un nid de flammes.

Que de malices dans l'attention dans la campagne ... Satan, Ferdinand, court avec les graines sauvages ... Jésus marche sur les ronces purpurines, sans les courber ... Jésus marchait sur les eaux irritées. La lanterne nous le montra debout, blanc et des tresses brunes, au flanc d'une vague d'émeraude ...

Je vais dévoiler tous les mystères: mystères religieux ou naturels, mort, naissance, avenir, passé, cosmogonie, néant. Je suis maître en fantasmagories.

Écoutez! ...

J'ai tous les talents! – Il n'y a personne ici et il y a quelqu'un: je ne voudrais pas répandre mon trésor. – Veut-on des chants nègres, des danses de houris? Veut-on que je disparaisse, que je plonge à la recherche de l'*anneau*? Veut-on? Je ferai de l'or, des remèdes.

Fiez-vous donc à moi, la foi soulage, guide, guérit. Tous, venez, – même les petits enfants, – que je vous console, qu'on répande pour vous son cœur, – le cœur merveilleux! – Pauvres hommes, travailleurs! Je ne demande pas de prières; avec votre confiance seulement, je serai heureux.

– Et pensons à moi. Ceci me fait peu regretter le monde. J'ai de la chance de ne pas souffrir plus. Ma vie ne fut que folies douces, c'est regrettable.

Bah! faisons toutes les grimaces imaginables.

Décidément, nous sommes hors du monde. Plus aucun son. Mon tact a disparu. Ah! mon château, ma Saxe, mon bois de saules. Les soirs, les matins, les nuits, les jours ... Suis-je las!

Je devrais avoir mon enfer pour la colère, mon enfer pour l'orgueil, – et l'enfer de la caresse; un concert d'enfers.

anyone else. Keep away from me. I must stink of burning flesh, I'm certain of it.

The hallucinations go on for ever. It has always been like that: the end of my faith in history, the neglect of principles. I'll say no more: poets and visionaries would be jealous. I am a thousand times the richer than they and I'll hoard it up like the sea.

And look at *this*! the clock of life has just ticked to a halt. I am no longer part of the world. – Theology means what it says, hell is certainly *down below* – and heaven up above. – Ecstasy, nightmare, sleep in a nest of flames.

What tricks the mind plays in the country ... Satan, Old Nick, blows about with the wild seed ... Jesus walks on the crimson thorns, without bending them ... Jesus once walked on the troubled waters. In the light of the lantern we saw him standing there, in white and with long brown hair, in the curve of an emerald wave ...

I am about to unveil all the mysteries: mysteries of religion or of nature, death, birth, the future, the past, cosmogony, extinction. I am a master of phantasmagoria.

Listen! ...

I can do everything! – There is no one here and there is someone here: I don't want to spill out all my treasured secrets. – What do you want? Negro chants? Arabian dancing-girls? Do you want me to disappear, to dive in search of the *ring*? Is that what you want? I shall fabricate gold, and remedies.

So trust me. Faith is soothing, it guides and heals. Come unto me, all of you – even the little children – and let me give you consolation, let a man put his heart out to you, – the wonderful heart! – Poor men and labourers! I do not ask for your prayers: your trust will be enough and I shall be happy.

Now let's think of me. All this does little to make me regret the world. I am fortunate not to suffer any longer. My life was spent in sweet stupidities – a pity.

Bah! I'll pull all the ugly faces I can.

There's no doubt about it, we have left the world behind. Not a sound left. My sense of touch has gone. Ah! my castle, my Saxony, my willow wood. Evenings, mornings, nights, days ... I'm so tired!

I ought to have a hell for my anger, a hell for my pride, – and a hell for embraces; a whole symphony of hells.

Je meurs de lassitude. C'est le tombeau, je m'en vais aux vers, horreur de l'horreur! Satan, farceur, tu veux me dissoudre, avec tes charmes. Je réclame. Je réclame! un coup de fourche, une goutte de feu.

Ah! remonter à la vie! Jeter les yeux sur nos difformités. Et ce poison, ce baiser mille fois maudit! Ma faiblesse, la cruauté du monde! Mon Dieu, pitié, cachez-moi, je me tiens trop mal! – Je suis caché et je ne le suis pas.

C'est le feu qui se relève avec son damné.

I am dying of fatigue. This is the grave, I am leaving for the worms, horror of horrors! Satan, you clown, you want to destroy me, with your enchantments. That is what I want. I crave for it! stab me with your pitchfork, sprinkle me with fire.

Ah! to return to life! To set eyes upon our deformities. And the poison, that utterly accursed kiss! My weakness, the cruelty of the world! My God, take pity, hide me, I cannot defend myself well enough! – I am hidden and I am not.

And the flames rise up with the damned soul.

DÉLIRES I

VIERGE FOLLE
L'ÉPOUX INFERNAL

Écoutons la confession d'un compagnon d'enfer:

«Ô divin Époux, mon Seigneur, ne refusez pas la confession de la plus triste de vos servantes. Je suis perdue. Je suis soûle. Je suis impure. Quelle vie!

«Pardon; divin Seigneur, pardon! Ah! pardon! Que de larmes! Et que de larmes encore plus tard, j'espère!

«Plus tard, je connaîtrai le divin Époux! Je suis née soumise à Lui. – L'autre peut me battre maintenant!

«A présent, je suis au fond du monde! Ô mes amies! ... non, pas mes amies ... Jamais délires ni tortures semblables ... Est-ce bête!

«Ah! je souffre, je crie. Je souffre vraiment. Tout pourtant m'est permis, chargée du mépris des plus méprisables cœurs.

«Enfin, faisons cette confidence, quitte à la répéter vingt autres fois, – aussi morne, aussi insignifiante!

«Je suis esclave de l'Époux infernal, celui qui a perdu les vierges folles. C'est bien ce démon-là. Ce n'est pas un spectre, ce n'est pas un fantôme. Mais moi qui ai perdu la sagesse, qui suis damnée et morte au monde, – on ne me tuera pas! – Comment vous le décrire! Je ne sais même plus parler. Je suis en deuil, je pleure, j'ai peur. Un peu de fraîcheur, Seigneur, si vous voulez, si vous voulez bien!

«Je suis veuve ... – J'étais veuve ... – mais oui, j'ai été bien sérieuse jadis, et je ne suis pas née pour devenir squelette! ... – Lui était presque un enfant ... Ses délicatesses mystérieuses m'avaient séduite. J'ai oublié tout mon devoir humain pour le suivre. Quelle vie! La vraie vie est absente. Nous ne sommes pas au monde. Je vais où il va, il le faut. Et souvent il s'emporte contre moi, *moi, la pauvre âme*. Le Démon! – C'est un Démon, vous savez, *ce n'est pas un homme*.

FIRST DELIRIUM

THE FOOLISH VIRGIN[5]
THE INFERNAL BRIDEGROOM

Let us listen to the confession of a companion in hell:

'O my Lord, heavenly Bridegroom, do not disdain the confession of the most miserable of your handmaidens. I am undone. I am drunk. I am unclean. What a life!

'Forgive me; O Lord in heaven, forgive me! Ah! forgive me! How I weep! and how much more weeping there is to come, I hope!

'In time I shall come to know the heavenly Bridegroom! I was born His servant. – For the present, the other one can beat me!

'Right now, I've sunk to the depths! Oh, my women friends! . . . no, not my friends . . . Never was there madness nor torment like this . . . It doesn't make sense!

'Oh, I'm in pain, I'm screaming from it. I really am in pain. I've a right to do whatever I want, now that I'm an object of contempt for the most contemptible feelings in people.

'So, let me make this confession, even if I have to repeat it twenty times over, – it's so dreary, so trivial!

'I am a slave of the infernal Bridegroom, the one who was the undoing of the foolish virgins. He is the devil I am talking about. He's no spectre, no ghost. But as one who has lost her mind, who is damned and dead to the world – there is nothing left of me to kill! – I am at a loss to describe him to you! I can't even find words any more. I am in mourning, I weep, I am frightened. Some fresh air, Lord, if you'd be so very kind!

'I am a widow . . . – I was a widow . . . – and yes, I was very serious-minded in the past, and I was not put on this earth to become a skeleton! . . . – He was little more than a child . . . His mysterious refinement and consideration had won me over. I neglected all my human obligations for him. What a life this is! Life lacks any reality. We are not in the real world. I follow him everywhere, I have no choice. And often he loses his temper with me, me, *poor soul that I am*. What a Devil! – He *is* a Devil, you know, *he's not a human being*.

«Il dit: «Je n'aime pas les femmes. L'amour est à réinventer, on le sait. Elles ne peuvent plus que vouloir une position assurée. La position gagnée, cœur et beauté sont mis de côté: il ne reste que froid dédain, l'aliment du mariage, aujourd'hui. Ou bien je vois des femmes, avec les signes du bonheur, dont, moi, j'aurai pu faire de bonnes camarades, dévorées tout d'abord par des brutes sensibles comme des bûchers . . .»

«Je l'écoute faisant de l'infamie une gloire, de la cruauté un charme. «Je suis de race lointaine: mes pères étaient Scandinaves: ils se perçaient les côtes, buvaient leur sang. — Je me ferai des entailles partout le corps, je me tatouerai, je veux devenir hideux comme un Mongol: tu verras, je hurlerai dans les rues. Je veux devenir bien fou de rage. Ne me montre jamais de bijoux, je ramperais et me tordrais sur le tapis. Ma richesse, je la voudrais tachée de sang partout. Jamais je ne travaillerai . . .» Plusieurs nuits, son démon me saisissant, nous nous roulions, je luttais avec lui! — Les nuits, souvents, ivre, il se poste dans des rues ou dans des maisons, pour m'épouvanter mortellement. — «On me coupera vraiment le cou; ce sera dégoûtant.» Oh! ces jours où il veut marcher avec l'air du crime!

«Parfois il parle, en une façon de patois attendri, de la mort qui fait repentir, des malheureux qui existent certainement, des travaux pénibles, des départs qui déchirent les cœurs. Dans les bouges où nous nous enivrions, il pleurait en considérant ceux qui nous entouraient, bétail de la misère. Il relevait les ivrognes dans les rues noires. Il avait la pitié d'une mère méchante pour les petits enfants. — Il s'en allait avec des gentillesses de petite fille au catéchisme. — Il feignait d'être éclairé sur tout, commerce, art, médecine. — Je le suivais, il le faut!

«Je voyais tout le décor dont, en esprit, il s'entourait; vêtements, draps, meubles: je lui prêtais des armes, une autre figure. Je voyais tout ce qui le touchait, comme il aurait voulu le créer pour lui. Quand il me semblait avoir l'esprit inerte, je le suivais, moi, dans des actions étranges et compliquées, loin, bonnes ou mauvaises: j'étais sûre de ne jamais entrer dans son monde. A côté de son cher corps endormi, que d'heures des nuits j'ai veillé, cherchant pourquoi il voulait tant s'évader de la réalité.

'He will say: "I don't love women. Love needs to be reinvented, it's obvious. Women are no longer capable of wanting anything but a secure life. Once that's achieved, feeling and beauty are forgotten: all that's left is cold disdain, the very stuff that marriage feeds on nowadays. Or else I come across women who have signs of happiness about them, with whom I could have had close companionship, and there they are, devoured from the outset by brutes who are about as sensitive as a pile of logs . . ."

'I listen to him turning infamy into honour, cruelty into a magic spell. "I go back a long way. My ancestors were Scandinavians: they pierced their sides, drank their blood. – I shall lacerate my whole body, I'll tattoo myself, I want to become as hideous as a Mongol: you'll see, I'll go screaming through the streets. I want to go really mad with rage. Don't ever show me jewels, or I'll crawl about the carpet in convulsions. I want my wealth to be stained all over with blood. I'll never do a day's work in my life . . ." Some nights, when I was seized by his evil spirit myself, we would roll about together, I would grapple with him! – At night, very often, drunk, he hides away somewhere in the streets or inside houses, so that he can scare me to death. "Someone really will slit my throat; it will be revolting." Oh! the days when he takes it into his head to walk about like a man bent on crime!

'Sometimes, adopting a kind of gentle patois, he talks about death bringing repentance, about the very real existence of the wretched, about the misery of some kinds of work, of heartrending leave-takings. In the dives where we got drunk, he used to weep when he noticed the people around us, the wretched cattle of humanity. He helped drunks to their feet in the dark streets. He showed the pity of a tough mother for tiny children. – He would walk away full of kind attention like a young girl coming from catechism class. He pretended he knew about everything, commerce, art, medicine. – I followed him, I have no choice!

'I could see all the trappings he set about him in his imagination; the costumes, drapes, furniture: I lent him weapons, a change of face. I could visualize everything that affected him, as he himself would have imagined it. Whenever I thought he was listless I would follow him into strange, complicated adventures, to the hilt, for good or bad: I knew I could never enter his world. As he slept, how many hours of the night I have lain sleepless beside his dear body, trying to imagine why he was so anxious to

Jamais homme n'eût pareil vœu. Je reconnaissais, – sans
craindre pour lui, – qu'il pouvait être un sérieux danger dans
la société. – Il a peut-être des secrets pour *changer la vie*? Non,
il ne fait qu'en chercher, me répliquais-je. Enfin sa charité est
ensorcelée, et j'en suis la prisonnière. Aucune autre âme n'au-
rait assez de force, – force de désespoir! – pour la supporter, –
pour être protégée et aimée par lui. D'ailleurs, je ne me le
figurais pas avec une autre âme: on voit son Ange, jamais
l'Ange d'un autre, – je crois. J'étais dans son âme comme dans
un palais qu'on a vidé pour ne pas voir une personne si peu
noble que vous: voilà tout. Hélas! je dépendais bien de lui.
Mais que voulait-il avec mon existence terne et lâche? Il ne me
rendait pas meilleure, s'il ne me faisait pas mourir! Tristement
dépitée, je lui dis quelquefois: «Je te comprends.» Il haussait
les épaules.

«Ainsi, mon chagrin se renouvelant sans cesse, et me trou-
vant plus égarée à mes yeux, – comme à tous les yeux qui
auraient voulu me fixer, si je n'eusse été condamnée pour
jamais à l'oubli de tous! – j'avais de plus en plus faim de sa
bonté. Avec ses baisers et ses étreintes amies, c'était bien un
ciel, un sombre ciel, où j'entrais, et où j'aurais voulu être
laissée, pauvre, sourde, muette, aveugle. Déjà j'en prenais l'ha-
bitude. Je nous voyais comme deux bons enfants, libres de se
promener dans le Paradis de tristesse. Nous nous accordions.
Bien émus, nous travaillions ensemble. Mais, après une péné-
trante caresse, il disait: «Comme ça te paraîtra drôle, quand je
n'y serai plus, ce par quoi tu as passé. Quand tu n'auras plus
mes bras sous ton cou, ni mon cœur pour t'y reposer, ni cette
bouche sur tes yeux. Parce qu'il faudra que je m'en aille, très-
loin, un jour. Puis il faut que j'en aide d'autres: c'est mon
devoir. Quoique ce ne soit guère ragoûtant . . ., chère âme . . .»
Tout de suite je me pressentais, lui parti, en proie au vertige,
précipitée dans l'ombre la plus affreuse: la mort. Je lui faisais
promettre qu'il ne me lâcherait pas. Il l'a faite vingt fois, cette
promesse d'amant. C'était aussi frivole que moi lui disant: «Je
te comprends.»

«Ah! je n'ai jamais été jalouse de lui. Il ne me quittera pas,
je crois. Que devenir? Il n'a pas une connaissance; il ne
travaillera jamais. Il veut vivre somnambule. Seules, sa bonté et
sa charité lui donneraient-elles droit dans le monde réel? Par

escape from reality. No man before ever had such a wish. I realized, – without being afraid for him, – that he could represent a serious threat to society. – Perhaps he has secrets that would *change the nature of life*? But no, he merely tries to discover them, I told myself. This charity of his is bewitched and I am its prisoner. No one else would have the strength, – the strength of despair! – to bear it, – to be cared for and loved by him. Besides, I could not imagine him being with anyone else: we see our own Angel, never other people's, – at least I think so. I lived in his soul as if it were a palace that had been emptied so that no one would see someone as unworthy as oneself: that is all there is to it. O God! I was really dependent on him. But what did he want with my spineless dull existence? He didn't improve me, even though he didn't manage to kill me! Sad and irritated, I sometimes said to him: "I understand you". He would shrug his shoulders.

'So with my heartache constantly renewed, and finding myself increasingly distraught, – as anybody would have done if they looked at me hard enough, had I not been condemned for ever to general neglect – I went on craving his affection more and more. His kisses and his friendly embraces were heaven, a dark heaven, and I entered it and would willingly have remained there, poor, deaf, dumb, blind. I was already getting used to it. I saw the two of us as happy children, free to wander in the Paradise of sorrow. We were in harmony with each other. With great emotion, we worked together. Yet, after some deeply affecting embrace, he would say: "How strange it will seem to you, when I'm not here any more, all that you have gone through. When you no longer feel my arms around your neck, nor my heart to rest on, nor my kisses on your eyes. Because I shall have to go away one day, very far away. There are others I have to help as well: that is my task. Not that I have any taste for it . . ., my darling . . ." And immediately I could imagine myself, with him gone, gripped by dizzy fear, hurled into the most horrible blackness: into death. I made him promise he wouldn't leave me. He made that lover's promise twenty times over. It was about as serious as me saying to him: "I understand you."

'Oh! I have never been jealous of him. I don't think he'll leave me. For what? He doesn't know a soul; he will never work. He wants to live like a sleepwalker. Are his kindness and charity enough to earn him a place in the real world? There are times

instants, j'oublie la pitié où je suis tombée: lui me rendra forte, nous voyagerons, nous chasserons dans les déserts, nous dor- mirons sur les pavés des villes inconnues, sans soins, sans peines. Ou je me réveillerai, et les lois et les mœurs auront changé, – grâce à son pouvoir magique, – le monde, en restant le même, me laissera à mes désirs, joies, nonchalances. Oh! la vie d'aventures qui existe dans les livres des enfants, pour me récompenser, j'ai tant souffert, me la donneras-tu? Il ne peut pas. J'ignore son idéal. Il m'a dit avoir des regrets, des espoirs: cela ne doit pas me regarder. Parle-t-il à Dieu? Peut-être devrais-je m'adresser à Dieu. Je suis au plus profond de l'abîme, et je ne sais plus prier.

«S'il m'expliquait ses tristesses, les comprendrais-je plus que ses railleries? Il m'attaque, il passe des heures à me faire honte de tout ce qui m'a pu toucher au monde, et s'indigne si je pleure.

« – Tu vois cet élégant jeune homme, entrant dans la belle et calme maison: il s'appelle Duval, Dufour, Armand, Maurice, que sais-je? Une femme s'est dévouée à aimer ce méchant idiot: elle est morte, c'est certes une sainte au ciel, à présent. Tu me feras mourir comme il a fait mourir cette femme. C'est notre sort, à nous, cœurs charitables . . .» Hélas! il avait des jours où tous les hommes agissant lui paraissaient les jouets de délires grotesques: il riait affreusement, longtemps. – Puis, il reprenait ses manières de jeune mère, de sœur aimée. S'il était moins sauvage, nous serions sauvés! Mais sa douceur aussi est mor- telle. Je lui suis soumise. – Ah! je suis folle!

«Un jour peut-être il disparaîtra merveilleusement; mais il faut que je sache, s'il doit remonter à un ciel, que je voie un peu l'assomption de mon petit ami!»

Drôle de ménage!

when I forget the pitiable mess I am in: he will make me strong,
we'll travel, we'll go hunting in unexplored territory, we'll sleep
on the pavements of unknown cities, carefree and happy. Or I
shall wake up to find laws and morals changed through his
magic power, – the world, though still the same, will leave me
to my desires, my joys and my lack of concern. Oh! that world
of adventure from children's books, won't you give it to me as
a reward? I've suffered so much. He cannot. I don't know what
his ideal world would be. He has told me of his regrets, his
hopes: but I'm not part of them. Does he speak to God? Perhaps
I ought to turn to God. I am in the very depths of the abyss,
and I have forgotten how to pray.

'If he were to explain what makes him miserable, would I under-
stand it any better than I do his scoffing remarks? He attacks me,
he spends hours making me feel ashamed of everything that has
ever meant something to me, then gets angry if I weep.

' " – You see that fashionable young man going into the lovely
peaceful house: his name is Duval, Dufour, Armand, Maurice, or
something. Some woman has devoted her time to loving that evil
fool: she is dead now, undoubtedly a saint in heaven. You'll be the
death of me in the same way as he was the death of that woman.
That is what awaits those of us who have unselfish hearts . . ." Oh
God! there were days when he saw all men alive as the puppets of
grotesque delirium: he would laugh horribly, on and on. – Then
he would go back to behaving like a young mother, a favourite
sister. Were he less wild, we would be saved! But even his
gentleness is deadly. I am in his power. – This is driving me mad!

'Perhaps one day he will just disappear by some miracle; but
I must be told about it, if he is to go to some kind of heaven, I
must get a glimpse of the assumption of my sweet young friend!'

A queer couple!

DÉLIRES II

ALCHIMIE DU VERBE

A moi. L'histoire d'une de mes folies.

Depuis longtemps je me vantais de posséder tous les paysages possibles, et trouvais dérisoires les célébrités de la peinture et de la poésie moderne.

J'aimais les peintures idiotes, dessus de portes, décors, toiles de saltimbanques, enseignes, enluminures populaires; la littérature démodée, latin d'église, livres érotiques sans orthographe, romans de nos aïeules, contes de fées, petits livres de l'enfance, opéras vieux, refrains niais, rhythmes naïfs.

Je rêvais croisades, voyages de découvertes dont on n'a pas de relations, républiques sans histoires, guerres de religion étouffées, révolutions de mœurs, déplacements de races et de continents: je croyais à tous les enchantements.

J'inventai la couleur des voyelles! – *A* noir, *E* blanc, *I* rouge, *O* bleu, *U* vert. – Je réglai la forme et le mouvement de chaque consonne, et, avec des rhythmes instinctifs, je me flattai d'inventer un verbe poétique accessible, un jour ou l'autre, à tous les sens. Je réservais la traduction.

Ce fut d'abord une étude. J'écrivais des silences, des nuits, je notais l'inexprimable. Je fixais des vertiges.

> Loin des oiseaux, des troupeaux, des villageoises,
> Que buvais-je, à genoux dans cette bruyère
> Entourée de tendres bois de noisetiers,
> Dans un brouillard d'après-midi tiède et vert?
>
> Que pouvais-je boire dans cette jeune Oise,
> – Ormeaux sans voix, gazon sans fleurs, ciel couvert! –
> Boire à ces gourdes jaunes, loin de ma case
> Chérie? Quelque liqueur d'or qui fait suer.
>
> Je faisais une louche enseigne d'auberge.
> – Un orage vint chasser le ciel. Au soir

SECOND DELIRIUM

ALCHEMY OF THE WORD

My turn now. The account of one of my insanities.

I had long boasted that every imaginable scene was in my grasp, and vented my scorn on the acclaimed masters of modern painting and poetry.

I had a taste for absurd paintings, the signs above doorways, stage scenery, the backdrops used by strolling players, inn-signs, cheap coloured prints; unfashionable literature, church Latin, erotic books with spelling-mistakes, novels our grandmothers read, fairy-tales, little books for children, old operas, meaningless refrains, obvious rhythms.

I dreamed about crusades, unrecorded voyages of discovery, republics with no history, repressed wars of religion, revolutions in manners, shifting races and continents: every piece of magic you can name – I believed in it.

I invented colours for vowels! – *A* black, *E* white, *I* red, *O* blue, *U* green. – I regulated the form and mobility of every consonant and, using an instinctive sense of rhythm, I flattered myself that I could invent a poetic language that would eventually be accessible to all the senses. I was less forthcoming putting it into practice.

At first it was an exercise. I wrote down silences, darkness, I noted down things that cannot be expressed. I pinned down vertigo.

> Far from birds and cattle and village girls
> What was I drinking, kneeling in heather
> Surrounded by young hazels in a wood,
> In the warm green mist of afternoon?
>
> What could I be drinking from the young Oise,
> – Voiceless elms, grass with no flowers, overcast sky! –
> What drink from those yellow gourds, far from the hut
> I loved? Some golden liquor that causes sweat.
>
> I seemed a dubious signboard for an inn.
> – A storm set in and chased away the sky. That evening

L'eau des bois se perdait sur les sables vierges,
Le vent de Dieu jetait des glaçons aux mares;

Pleurant, je voyais de l'or – et ne pus boire. –

———

A quatre heures du matin, l'été,
Le sommeil d'amour dure encore.
Sous les bocages s'évapore
   L'odeur du soir fêté.

Là-bas, dans leur vaste chantier
Au soleil des Hespérides,
Déjà s'agitent – en bras de chemise –
   Les Charpentiers.

Dans leurs Déserts de mousse, tranquilles,
Ils préparent les lambris précieux
    Où la ville
   Peindra de faux cieux.

Ô, pour ces Ouvriers charmants
Sujets d'un roi de Babylone,
Vénus! quitte un instant les Amants
Dont l'âme est en couronne.

  Ô Reine des Bergers,
Porte aux travailleurs l'eau-de-vie,
Que leurs forces soient en paix
En attendant le bain dans la mer à midi.

La vieillerie poétique avait une bonne part dans mon alchimie du verbe.

Je m'habituai à l'hallucination simple: je voyais très-franchement une mosquée à la place d'une usine, une école de tambours faite par des anges, des calèches sur les routes du ciel, un salon au fond d'un lac; les monstres, les mystères; un titre de vaudeville dressait des épouvantes devant moi.

Puis j'expliquai mes sophismes magiques avec l'hallucination des mots!

Je finis par trouver sacré le désordre de mon esprit. J'étais oisif, en proie à une lourde fièvre: j'enviais la félicité des bêtes,

Water from the woods trickled away on virgin sands,
God's wind hurled ice upon the ponds;

I saw gold through my tears – but could not drink.

———

Four o'clock, a summer morning,
And love still lying there asleep.
The scents of last night's revelry
Fade beneath copses.

Down there in the vast work-yard lit
By the Hesperidean sun,
The Carpenters in shirtsleeves
Already start to stir.

At peace in their mossy Deserts,
They work on the costly panels
Which the city will paint
With artificial skies.

For these workmen, for the charming
Subjects of some king of Babylon,
O Venus! leave the Lovers for a second
And their haloed souls.

O Queen of the Shepherds,
Bring brandy to these workers,
And so rest their strength until
They bathe at midday in the sea.

Outmoded ideas of poetry played an important part in my alchemy of the word.

I accustomed myself to simple forms of hallucination: I would actually see a mosque where there was a factory, a drummers' corps composed of angels, coaches on the roads in the sky, a drawing-room at the bottom of a lake; monsters, mysteries; a music-hall billboard could conjure up horrors right there in front of me.

And I explained my magic sophisms by making words hallucinatory!

I eventually came to see the disorder of my mind as sacred. I idled away my time, a prey to oppressive fever: I envied the

– les chenilles, qui représentent l'innocence des limbes, les taupes, le sommeil de la virginité!

Mon caractère s'aigrissait. Je disais adieu au monde dans d'espèces de romances:

CHANSON DE LA PLUS HAUTE TOUR

> Qu'il vienne, qu'il vienne,
> Le temps dont on s'éprenne.

> J'ai tant fait patience
> Qu'à jamais j'oublie.
> Craintes et souffrances
> Aux cieux sont parties.
> Et la soif malsaine
> Obscurcit mes veines.

> Qu'il vienne, qu'il vienne,
> Le temps dont on s'éprenne.

> Telle la prairie
> A l'oubli livrée,
> Grandie, et fleurie
> D'encens et d'ivraies,
> Au bourdon farouche
> Des sales mouches.

> Qu'il vienne, qu'il vienne,
> Le temps dont on s'éprenne.

J'aimai le désert, les vergers brûlés, les boutiques fanées, les boissons tiédies. Je me traînais dans les ruelles puantes et, les yeux fermés, je m'offrais au soleil, dieu de feu.

«Général, s'il reste un vieux canon sur tes remparts en ruines, bombarde-nous avec des blocs de terre sèche. Aux glaces des magasins splendides! dans les salons! Fais manger sa poussière à la ville. Oxyde les gargouilles. Emplis les boudoirs de poudre de rubis brûlante ...»

Oh! le moucheron enivré à la pissotière de l'auberge, amoureux de la bourrache, et que dissout un rayon!

happy state of animals – caterpillars, who represent the inno-
cence of limbo, and moles, the sleep of virginity!

My character turned sour. I took my farewell of the world
in kinds of sentimental ballads:

SONG OF THE HIGHEST TOWER

Let it come, let it come,
The age we could love.

I have waited so long
And memory is gone.
The fears and the hurts
Have fled to the skies.
And morbid desires
Are darkening my blood.

Let it come, let it come,
The age we could love.

Like the green field
Fallen to neglect,
Grown high and in flower
With incense and weeds.
In the harsh buzzing
Of the filthy flies.

Let it come, let it come,
The age we could love.

I loved abandoned places, burnt orchards, musty shops,
tepid drinks. I would drag myself through stinking alleys,
close my eyes, and offer myself up to the sun, god of fire.

'General, if you have an old cannon left on those ruined
ramparts, bombard us with clods of dried earth. Shatter the
mirrors of luxury shops! Fire on the drawing-rooms! Make
the city swallow its own dust. Rust the water conduits. Fill
the boudoirs with blazing ruby powder . . .'

Oh! the little fly, drunk in the piss-house of a country inn,
besotted with borage, and dissolved in a ray of sunlight!

FAIM

Si j'ai du goût, ce n'est guère
Que pour la terre et les pierres.
Je déjeune toujours d'air,
De roc, de charbons, de fer.

Mes faims, tournez. Paissez, faims,
  Le pré des sons.
Attirez le gai venin
  Des liserons.

Mangez les cailloux qu'on brise,
Les vieilles pierres d'églises;
Les galets des vieux déluges,
Pains semés dans les vallées grises.

————

Le loup criait sous les feuilles
En crachant les belles plumes
De son repas de volailles:
Comme lui je me consume.

Les salades, les fruits
N'attendent que la cueillette;
Mais l'araignée de la haie
Ne mange que des violettes.

Que je dorme! que je bouille
Aux autels de Salomon.
Le bouillon court sur la rouille,
Et se mêle au Cédron.

Enfin, ô bonheur, ô raison, j'écartai du ciel l'azur, qui est du noir, et je vécus, étincelle d'or de la lumière *nature*. De joie, je prenais une expression bouffonne et égarée au possible:

Elle est retrouvée!
Quoi? l'éternité.
C'est la mer mêlée
Au soleil.

HUNGER

What taste I have
Is for earth and stones.
I always feed on air,
On rocks, on iron and coals.

Hungers, turn. Hungers, feed
On fields of bran.
Gather the bright poison
Of convolvulus.

Eat the broken stones,
The old stone of churches;
Pebbles from ancient floods,
Bread sown in the grey valleys.

———

Beneath the bushes howled the wolf
Spitting out fine feathers
From his feast of fowl:
And I, likewise, devour myself.

Salads and fruits
Are there for the picking:
But the hedge spider
Will only eat the violets.

Let me sleep! let me boil
On the altars of Solomon.
The broth spills over the rust
And flows into the Kedron.[6]

Finally – with what a blissful sense of reason! – I removed
from the sky the blue that is a blackness, and I lived as a
golden spark of *natural* light. In my delight I adopted as
clownish and distraught a form of expression as possible:

Rediscovered once more?
Ah yes! eternity:
The mingled light
Of sun and sea.

Mon âme éternelle,
Observe ton vœu
Malgré la nuit seule
Et le jour en feu.

Donc tu te dégages
Des humains suffrages,
Des communs élans!
Tu voles selon ...

– Jamais l'espérance.
     Pas d'*orietur*.
Science et patience,
Le supplice est sûr.

Plus de lendemain,
Braises de satin,
     Votre ardeur
     Est le devoir.

Elle est retrouvée!
– Quoi? – l'Éternité.
C'est la mer mêlée
     Au soleil.

Je devins un opéra fabuleux: je vis que tous les êtres ont une fatalité de bonheur: l'action n'est pas la vie, mais une façon de gâcher quelque force, un énervement. La morale est la faiblesse de la cervelle.

A chaque être, plusieurs *autres* vies me semblaient dues. Ce monsieur ne sait ce qu'il fait: il est un ange. Cette famille est une nichée de chiens. Devant plusieurs hommes, je causai tout haut avec un moment d'une de leurs autres vies. – Ainsi, j'ai aimé un porc.

Aucun des sophismes de la folie, – la folie qu'on enferme, – n'a été oublié par moi: je pourrais les redire tous, je tiens le système.

Ma santé fut menacée. La terreur venait. Je tombais dans des sommeils de plusieurs jours, et, levé, je continuais les rêves les plus tristes. J'étais mûr pour le trépas, et par une route de dangers ma faiblesse me menait aux confins du monde et de la Cimmérie, patrie de l'ombre et des tourbillons.

Observe your vow,
Eternal soul,
Despite the lone night
And burning day.

Then you are free
From human right
And common aim!
And so you fly . . .

– No hope is left.
No *orietur*.[7]
Knowledge, endurance,
Torment assured.

No coming day,
Embers of silk,
Your heat alone
Is duty done.

Rediscovered once more?
Ah yes! eternity.
The mingled light
Of sun and sea.

I became a fabulous opera: I saw that every being is fated to
seek happiness: action is not life but a way of ruining a source
of strength, a restlessness of the nerves. Morality is the weakness
of the brain.

To every being, it seemed to me, several *other* lives were due.
This gentleman doesn't know what he's doing: he is an angel.
This family is a litter of dogs. In the presence of several men, I
conversed out loud with a moment of one of their other lives. –
That's how I came to love a pig.

Not one of the illogicalities of madness – the sort of madness
that gets locked up – did I overlook: I could repeat every one of
them, I know them backwards.

My health became endangered. Terror was imminent. I fell
into sleep for days at a time, and when I awoke the saddest
dreams persisted. I was ripe for death, and my weakness led me
down dangerous paths to the ends of the earth, to the borders
of Cimmeria,[8] the home of shadow and whirlwinds.

Je dus voyager, distraire les enchantements assemblés sur mon cerveau. Sur la mer, que j'aimais comme si elle eût dû me laver d'une souillure, je voyais se lever la croix consolatrice. J'avais été damné par l'arc-en-ciel. Le Bonheur était ma fatalité, mon remords, mon ver: ma vie serait toujours trop immense pour être dévouée à la force et à la beauté.

Le Bonheur! Sa dent, douce à la mort, m'avertissait au chant du coq, – *ad matutinum*, au *Christus venit*, – dans les plus sombres villes:

> Ô saisons, ô châteaux!
> Quelle âme est sans défauts?
>
> J'ai fait la magique étude
> Du bonheur, qu'aucun n'élude.
>
> Salut à lui, chaque fois
> Que chante le coq gaulois.
>
> Ah! je n'aurai plus d'envie:
> Il s'est chargé de ma vie.
>
> Ce charme a pris âme et corps
> Et dispersé les efforts.
>
> Ô saisons, ô chateaux!
>
> L'heure de sa fuite, hélas!
> Sera l'heure du trépas.
>
> Ô saisons, ô chateaux!

Cela s'est passé. Je sais aujourd'hui saluer la beauté.

I was forced to travel, to dispel the enchantments sitting on my brain. Over the sea, which I loved as the thing that would wash me clean of defilement, I saw the cross of consolation rise. I had been damned by the rainbow. Happiness was my fate, my remorse, my worm: my life would always far exceed a devotion to strength and beauty.

Happiness! Its bite, sweet unto death, alerted me at cock crow – *ad matutinum*, at the *Christus venit*,[9] – in the darkest of cities:

> Seasons, castles!
> Where is a flawless soul?
>
> I studied the magic
> Of happiness no one avoids.
>
> I greet it whenever
> The Gallic cock crows.
>
> I shall never want again!
> It has taken charge of my life.
>
> The spell has taken body and soul
> And dispersed all effort.
>
> Seasons, castles!
>
> The evil day it disappears
> Will be the day of death.
>
> Seasons, castles!

All that is over. Today, I know what salutation beauty deserves.

L'IMPOSSIBLE

Ah! cette vie de mon enfance, la grande route par tous les temps, sobre surnaturellement, plus désintéressé que le meilleur des mendiants, fier de n'avoir ni pays, ni amis, quelle sottise c'était. – Et je m'en aperçois seulement!

– J'ai eu raison de mépriser ces bonshommes qui ne perdraient pas l'occasion d'une caresse, parasites de la propreté et de la santé de nos femmes, aujourd'hui qu'elles sont si peu d'accord avec nous.

J'ai eu raison dans tous mes dédains: puisque je m'évade!

Je m'évade!

Je m'explique.

Hier encore, je soupirais: «Ciel! sommes-nous assez de damnés ici-bas! Moi j'ai tant de temps déjà dans leur troupe! Je les connais tous. Nous nous reconnaissons toujours; nous nous dégoûtons. La charité nous est inconnue. Mais nous sommes polis; nos relations avec le monde sont très-convenables.» Est-ce étonnant? Le monde! les marchands, les naïfs! – Nous ne sommes pas déshonorés. – Mais les élus, comment nous recevraient-ils? Or il y a des gens hargneux et joyeux, de faux élus, puisqu'il nous faut de l'audace ou de l'humilité pour les aborder. Ce sont les seuls élus. Ce ne sont pas des bénisseurs!

M'étant retrouvé deux sous de raison – ça passe vite! – je vois que mes malaises viennent de ne m'être pas figuré assez tôt que nous sommes à l'Occident. Les marais occidentaux! Non que je croie la lumière altérée, la forme exténuée, le mouvement égaré ... Bon! voici que mon esprit veut absolument se charger de tous les développements cruels qu'a subis l'esprit depuis la fin de l'Orient ... Il en veut, mon esprit!

... Mes deux sous de raison sont finis! – L'esprit est autorité, il veut que je sois en Occident. Il faudrait le faire taire pour conclure comme je voulais.

J'envoyais au diable les palmes des martyrs, les rayons de l'art, l'orgueil des inventeurs, l'ardeur des pillards; je retournais

IMPOSSIBILITY

Ah! that life of my childhood, the open road in all weathers, supernatural sobriety, less bothered what would happen to me than the most experienced beggar, proud to have neither country, norfriends, what foolishness it was. – And only now do I realize it!

– I was right to scorn those fellows who never miss the chance of a kiss, parasites on the cleanliness and health of our women, when women today are so little in accord with men.

I was right in everything I scorned: because I am leaving it all behind!

Taking to my heels!

Let me explain.

Only yesterday I kept sighing: 'God! there are surely enough of us, the damned souls on the earth! I've been among them long enough! I know every one of them. We never fail to recognize each other; we disgust each other. Charity isn't a word we recognize. Still, we're polite enough; our dealings with people are more than decent.' Is there anything surprising about that! Did I say people! Tradesmen and dolts! – We have not disgraced ourselves. – But the elect, what kind of welcome would *they* give us? Now there are surly people, joyful people, and they are a false elect, since it takes either audacity or meekness to approach them. These are the only elect we have. They've no blessings to spare!

Back in my right mind, all twopence worth of it – it's soon enough spent! – I can see that my disquiets stem from the fact that I was not quick enough to realize that we live in the Western world. These Western swamps! Not that I think that the light is impaired, that forms are worn out, or activities misguided . . . So! my mind is avid to concern itself with all the evil developments imposed upon the mind since the collapse of the Orient . . . It has a grudge to bear, my mind!

. . . So much for my twopence worth of reason! – The mind is authority, it wants me in the West. It would have to be silenced for me to draw the conclusions I wanted.

I used to say to hell with martyrs' palms, with the light cast by art, the pride of inventors, the frenzy of plunderers; I turned

à l'Orient et à la sagesse première et éternelle. – Il paraît que c'est un rêve de paresse grossière!

Pourtant, je ne songeais guère au plaisir d'échapper aux souffrances modernes. Je n'avais pas en vue la sagesse bâtarde du Coran. – Mais n'y a-t-il pas un supplice réel en ce que, depuis cette déclaration de la science, le christianisme, l'homme *se joue*, se prouve les évidences, se gonfle du plaisir de répéter ces preuves, et ne vit que comme cela! Torture subtile, niaise; source de mes divagations spirituelles. La nature pourrait s'ennuyer, peut-être! M. Prudhomme est né avec le Christ.

N'est-ce pas parce que nous cultivons la brume! Nous mangeons la fièvre avec nos légumes aqueux. Et l'ivrognerie! et le tabac! et l'ignorance! et les dévouements! – Tout cela est-il assez loin de la pensée de la sagesse de l'Orient, la patrie primitive? Pourquoi un monde moderne, si de pareils poisons s'inventent!

Les gens d'Église diront: C'est compris. Mais vous voulez parler de l'Éden. Rien pour vous dans l'histoire des peuples orientaux. – C'est vrai; c'est à l'Éden que je songeais! Qu'est-ce que c'est pour mon rêve, cette pureté des races antiques!

Les philosophes: Le monde n'a pas d'âge. L'humanité se déplace, simplement. Vous êtes en Occident, mais libre d'habiter dans votre Orient, quelque ancien qu'il vous le faille, – et d'y habiter bien. Ne soyez pas un vaincu. Philosophes, vous êtes de votre Occident.

Mon esprit, prends garde. Pas de partis de salut violents. Exerce-toi! – Ah! la science ne va pas assez vite pour nous!

– Mais je m'aperçois que mon esprit dort.

S'il était bien éveillé toujours à partir de ce moment, nous serions bientôt à la vérité, qui peut-être nous entoure avec ses anges pleurant!... – S'il avait été éveillé jusqu'à ce moment-ci, c'est que je n'aurais pas cédé aux instincts délétères, à une époque immémoriale!... – S'il avait toujours été bien éveillé, je voguerais en pleine sagesse!...

Ô pureté! pureté!

C'est cette minute d'éveil qui m'a donné la vision de la pureté! – Par l'esprit on va à Dieu!

Déchirante infortune!

back to the Orient and to original, eternal wisdom. – It seems that this is a crude and lazy-minded dream!

Yet I was hardly dreaming of a pleasurable escape from present suffering. The hybrid wisdom of the Koran was not what I had in mind. – But is there not real torture in the fact that since that declaration of science, Christianity, man has been deceiving himself, proving the obvious to himself, bursting with pride as he goes on repeating the proofs, as his only way of life! A subtle, mindless form of torture; the source of my spiritual ramblings. Nature could well get bored! Mr Know-All was born along with Jesus Christ.

Isn't this because we go out of our way to live in a fog? We digest fever with our watery vegetables. And alcohol! and tobacco! and ignorance! and blind faith! – Isn't it all a bit far from the thought and the wisdom of the Orient, our original birth-place? Why have a modern world if such poisons are invented!

People of the Church will say: Of course. But you are really talking about Eden. There is nothing for you in the history of Oriental civilization. – Yes, yes; it was Eden that I meant! What does the purity of ancient races have to do with my dream!

The philosophers will say: The world has no age. Humanity moves from place to place, that is all. You live in the Western world, but you're free to live in your Orient, as old an Orient as you need, – and to live in it comfortably. Don't be a defeatist. Philosophers, you belong to your Western world.

My mind, be careful. No wild bids for salvation. Keep alert! – Ah! science never moves fast enough for us!

– But I see that my mind is asleep.

Were it to stay wide awake from this moment on, we would soon reach the truth which may even now surround us, with its angels weeping! . . . If it had been awake up to this moment, then I should not have given in to pernicious instincts, to the idea of a long-lost time! . . . If it had always been wide awake, I would be floating on total wisdom! . . .

Purity! purity!

It is this minute of wakefulness that has given me the vision of purity! – The mind leads to God!

What agonizing misfortune!

L'ÉCLAIR

Le travail humain! c'est l'explosion qui éclaire mon abîme de temps en temps.

«Rien n'est vanité; à la science, et en avant!» crie l'Ecclésiaste moderne, c'est-à-dire *Tout le monde*. Et pourtant les cadavres des méchants et des fainéants tombent sur le cœur des autres ... Ah! vite, vite un peu; là-bas, par delà la nuit, ces récompenses futures, éternelles ... les échappons-nous? ...

– Qu'y puis-je? Je connais le travail; et la science est trop lente. Que la prière galope et que la lumière gronde ... je le vois bien. C'est trop simple, et il fait trop chaud; on se passera de moi. J'ai mon devoir, j'en serai fier à la façon de plusieurs, en le mettant de côté.

Ma vie est usée. Allons! feignons, fainéantons, ô pitié! Et nous existerons en nous amusant, en rêvant amours monstres et univers fantastiques, en nous plaignant et en querellant les apparences du monde, saltimbanque, mendiant, artiste, bandit, – prêtre! Sur mon lit d'hôpital, l'odeur de l'encens m'est revenue si puissante; gardien des aromates sacrés, confesseur, martyr ...

Je reconnais là ma sale éducation d'enfance. Puis quoi! ... Aller mes vingt ans, si les autres vont vingt ans ...

Non! non! à présent je me révolte contre la mort! Le travail paraît trop léger à mon orgueil: ma trahison au monde serait un supplice trop court. Au dernier moment, j'attaquerais à droite, à gauche ...

Alors, – oh! – chère pauvre âme, l'éternité serait-elle pas perdue pour nous!

LIGHTNING

Human labour! the explosion that lights up my abyss from time to time.

'Nothing is vanity; strike on towards knowledge!' shouts the modern Ecclesiast, which means *Everybody*. And still the corpses of the wicked and the idle go on falling on the hearts of others . . . Ah! quick, come on, quick; over there, beyond the darkness, the eternal rewards to come . . . are we to miss out on them? . . .

– What can I do about it? I know what work is; and science is too slow. Let prayers go galloping and the light rumble away . . . I can see all that. It is too easy, and the weather's too hot; they can do without me. I have my duty, I'll be proud of it, like so many others, and just forget it.

My life is worn out. Right then! let's pretend, let's do nothing, for pity's sake! And we shall live by amusing ourselves, dreaming of monstrous loves and fantastic universes, complaining and attacking the ways of the world – clowns, beggars, artists, bandits, – priests! On my hospital bed, the smell of incense came back to me so powerfully; keeper of the holy aromatics, confessor, martyr . . .

I know where all that comes from: my foul childhood upbringing. So what! . . . Turn twenty, if everyone else is going to . . .

No! no! for the moment I rebel against death! Work seems too trivial a thing for pride like mine: to betray myself to the world would be too brief an ordeal. At the last moment I would strike out to right and left . . .

And then, – oh! – my blessed little soul, would eternity not be lost to us!

MATIN

N'eus-je pas *une fois* une jeunesse aimable, héroïque, fabuleuse, à écrire sur des feuilles d'or, – trop de chance! Par quel crime, par quelle erreur, ai-je mérité ma faiblesse actuelle? Vous qui prétendez que des bêtes poussent des sanglots de chagrin, que des malades désespèrent, que des morts rêvent mal, tâchez de raconter ma chute et mon sommeil. Moi, je ne puis pas plus m'expliquer que le mendiant avec ses continuels *Pater* et *Ave Maria. Je ne sais plus parler!*

Pourtant, aujourd'hui, je crois avoir fini la relation de mon enfer. C'était bien l'enfer; l'ancien, celui dont le fils de l'homme ouvrit les portes.

Du même désert, à la même nuit, toujours mes yeux las se réveillent à l'étoile d'argent, toujours, sans que s'émeuvent les Rois de la vie, les trois mages, le cœur, l'âme, l'esprit. Quand irons-nous, par delà les grèves et les monts, saluer la naissance du travail nouveau, la sagesse nouvelle, la fuite des tyrans et des démons, la fin de la superstition, adorer – les premiers! – Noël sur la terre!

Le chant des cieux, la marche des peuples! Esclaves, ne maudissons pas la vie.

MORNING

Did I not *once* have a pleasant young life, a heroic magical time to be written on sheets of gold, – no such luck! What crime, what fault brought me to my present state of weakness? You who claim that beasts can sob with grief, that the sick give up hope, that the dead have bad dreams, try now to give an account of my fall and my sleep. I can no more explain myself than a beggar with his string of *Pater nosters* and *Ave Marias. I no longer know how to speak!*

Yet today I think I have finished the account of my hell. It *was* hell; the ancient hell whose gates were opened by the Son of Man.

From the same desert, towards the same darkness, my weary eyes never fail to open to the silver star, without a sign from the Kings of life, the three wise men, the heart, the soul, the mind. When shall we go, beyond the mountains and the seashores, and hail the birth of the new labour, the new wisdom, the flight of despots and devils, the end of superstition, and be the first to worship Christmas on earth!

The song of the heavens, the march of nations! Slaves we are, but let us not curse our lives.

ADIEU

L'automne déjà! – Mais pourquoi regretter un éternel soleil, si nous sommes engagés à la découverte de la clarté divine, – loin des gens qui meurent sur les saisons.

L'automne. Notre barque élevée dans les brumes immobiles tourne vers le port de la misère, la cité énorme au ciel taché de feu et de boue. Ah! les haillons pourris, le pain trempé de pluie, l'ivresse, les mille amours qui m'ont crucifié! Elle ne finira donc point cette goule reine de millions d'âmes et de corps morts *et qui seront jugés!* Je me revois la peau rongée par la boue et la peste, des vers plein les cheveux et les aisselles et encore de plus gros vers dans le cœur, étendu parmi les inconnus sans âge, sans sentiment ... J'aurais pu y mourir ... L'affreuse évocation! J'exècre la misère.

Et je redoute l'hiver parce que c'est la saison du comfort!

– Quelquefois je vois au ciel des plages sans fin couvertes de blanches nations en joie. Un grand vaisseau d'or, au-dessus de moi, agite ses pavillons multicolores sous les brises du matin. J'ai créé toutes les fêtes, tous les triomphes, tous les drames. J'ai essayé d'inventer de nouvelles fleurs, de nouveaux astres, de nouvelles chairs, de nouvelles langues. J'ai cru acquérir des pouvoirs surnaturels. Eh bien! je dois enterrer mon imagination et mes souvenirs! Une belle gloire d'artiste et de conteur emportée!

Moi! moi qui me suis dit mage ou ange, dispensé de toute morale, je suis rendu au sol, avec un devoir à chercher, et la réalité rugueuse à étreindre! Paysan!

Suis-je trompé? la charité serait-elle sœur de la mort, pour moi?

Enfin, je demanderai pardon pour m'être nourri de mensonge. Et allons.

Mais pas une main amie! et où puiser le secours?

———

Oui l'heure nouvelle est au moins très-sévère.

Car je puis dire que la victoire m'est acquise: les grincements de dents, les sifflements de feu, les soupirs empestés se modèrent. Tous les souvenirs immondes s'effacent. Mes derniers regrets

ADIEU

Autumn so soon! – But why look back with regret to eternal sunshine when we are set to discover divine light, – far from people who die with the changing seasons.

Autumn. Our boat, high in the hanging mists, turns towards the harbour of poverty, the monstrous city, its sky stained with fire and filth. Ah! those stinking rags, the rain-soaked bread, the drunkenness, the thousand loves that crucified my life! Will she never have done, this vampire queen of a million dead souls and bodies *and they will be judged!* I can see myself there now, my skin pitted with dirt and plague, my hair and armpits crawling with worms, and still bigger worms in my heart, lying there with ageless, nameless people, unfeeling . . . I might have died there . . . A hideous thing to remember! I utterly loathe poverty!

And I dread winter because it is such a cosy season!

– Sometimes, in the sky, I see endless beaches thronging with exultant white nations. Above me, a great golden ship flutters its multicoloured pennants in the morning breezes. I have created every festivity, every triumph, every drama. I have tried to invent new flowers, new stars, new bodies, new languages. I thought I had acquired supernatural powers. Well! Now I need to bury my imagination and my memories! A fine end to fame as an artist and story-teller!

And here I am! I, who called myself a magus or an angel, exempt from all moral law, I am returned to the earth with a task to seek and coarse-grained truths to embrace! A peasant!

Am I wrong? is charity the sister of death in my case?

Well, I shall ask forgiveness for living on lies. Let's get on with it.

But not one helping hand? and where can I look for help?

———

It's true: this new era is nothing if not exacting.

What I can say is that I have gained a victory: the grinding of teeth, the hissing flames, the reeking sighs are subsiding. All the squalid memories are fading. My final regrets are on the run, –

détalent, – des jalousies pour les mendiants, les brigands, les amis de la mort, les arriérés de toutes sortes. – Damnés, si je me vengeais!

Il faut être absolument moderne.

Point de cantiques: tenir le pas gagné. Dure nuit! le sang séché fume sur ma face, et je n'ai rien derrière moi, que cet horrible arbrisseau! … Le combat spirituel est aussi brutal que la bataille d'hommes; mais la vision de la justice est le plaisir de Dieu seul.

Cependant c'est la veille. Recevons tous les influx de vigueur et de tendresse réelle. Et à l'aurore, armés d'une ardente patience, nous entrerons aux splendides villes.

Que parlais-je de main amie! Un bel avantage, c'est que je puis rire des vieilles amours mensongères, et frapper de honte ces couples menteurs, – j'ai vu l'enfer des femmes là-bas; – et il me sera loisible de *posséder la vérité dans une âme et un corps*.

Avril – août, 1873.

envy of beggars, bandits, those who court death, all sorts of backward creatures. – They would be damned, were I to take my revenge.

One needs to live utterly in the present.

No hymn-singing: hold on to any step forward. A hard night! the dried blood smokes on my face and there is nothing behind me but that horrible stunted tree! ... Spiritual struggle is as brutal as the battles of men; but the vision of justice is for God's eyes alone.

Yet this is the vigil. Let us welcome every influx of energy and real affection. And at dawn, armed with a strong sense of endurance, we shall enter the cities of splendour.

Why was I talking of a helping hand! I have the great advantage now of being able to laugh at the falsity of past loves and to strike shame into the deceits of coupledom, – I saw the hell of women down there; – and I shall now be at liberty *to possess truth within one soul and one body.*

April – August, 1873

NOTES TO
A Season in Hell

[1] Declaration of the Rights of Man: the founding document of the French Revolution and of the French republican tradition. The basic rights are freedom, property, security, and resistance to oppression.

[2] Solyma: Jerusalem.

[3] *De profundis Domine*: Psalms cxxx: 'Out of the depths have I cried unto thee, O Lord.'

[4] children of Ham: Ham, a son of Noah, is traditionally regarded as the ancestor of the black race.

[5] The allusion is to the parable of the Wise and Foolish Virgins (Matthew xxv.1–3). Of the ten virgins awaiting the Heavenly Bridegroom, five (the wise virgins) were prepared, five (the foolish virgins) were not and were therefore excluded from the Kingdom of Heaven. Rimbaud removes the parable from the Kingdom of Heaven and transfers it to Hell. 'First Delirium' is read by many commentators as a representation of the relationship between Rimbaud and Verlaine. While this may well be the case, the text has wider implications about the nature of coupledom.

[6] The Kedron Valley separates Jerusalem from the Mount of Olives, and the stream flows into the Dead Sea.

[7] *orietur*: 'there will arise'

[8] Cimmeria: the name that classical antiquity gave to the remotest ends of the earth, a land shrouded in darkness and close to the kingdom of the dead.

[9] The liturgical fragments ('in the morning', 'Christ is coming') from Sunday Lauds, together with the mention of cock-crow, suggest allusion to St Peter's denial of Christ and his subsequent repentance.

ILLUMINATIONS

APRÈS LE DÉLUGE

Aussitôt après que l'idée du Déluge se fut rassise,

Un lièvre s'arrêta dans les sainfoins et les clochettes mouvantes et dit sa prière à l'arc-en-ciel à travers la toile de l'araignée.

Oh! les pierres précieuses qui se cachaient, – les fleurs qui regardaient déjà.

Dans la grande rue sale les étals se dressèrent, et l'on tira les barques vers la mer étagée là-haut comme sur les gravures.

Le sang coula, chez Barbe-Bleue, – aux abattoirs, – dans les cirques, où le sceau de Dieu blêmit les fenêtres. Le sang et le lait coulèrent.

Les castors bâtirent. Les «mazagrans» fumèrent dans les estaminets.

Dans la grande maison de vitres encore ruisselante les enfants en deuil regardèrent les merveilleuses images.

Une porte claqua, et sur la place du hameau, l'enfant tourna ses bras, compris des girouettes et des coqs des clochers de partout, sous l'éclatante giboulée.

Madame *** établit un piano dans les Alpes. La messe et les premières communions se célébrèrent aux cent mille autels de la cathédrale.

Les caravanes partirent. Et le Splendide Hôtel fut bâti dans le chaos de glaces et de nuit du pôle.

Depuis lors, la Lune entendit les chacals piaulant par les déserts de thym, – et les églogues en sabots grognant dans le verger. Puis, dans la futaie violette, bourgeonnante, Eucharis me dit que c'était le printemps.

– Sourds, étang, – Écume, roule sur le pont, et par-dessus les bois; – draps noirs et orgues, – éclairs et tonnerre; – montez et roulez; – Eaux et tristesses, montez et relevez les Déluges.

Car depuis qu'ils se sont dissipés, – oh les pierres précieuses s'enfouissant, et les fleurs ouvertes! – c'est un ennui! et la Reine, la Sorcière qui allume sa braise dans le pot de terre, ne voudra jamais nous raconter ce qu'elle sait, et que nous ignorons.

AFTER THE FLOOD

Just as soon as the idea of the Flood had subsided,

A hare stopped amid the clover and the swaying flower-bells and said his prayer to the rainbow through the spider's web.

Oh! the precious gems that began to conceal themselves, – the flowers that were already opening their eyes to the world.

In the dirt of the high street stalls were set up, and boats were hauled down to the sea as it rose up in tiers as it does in old prints.

Blood flowed, at Bluebeard's, – in the slaughter-houses, – in circuses, where the seal of God turned the windows deathly pale. Blood flowed. Milk flowed.

The beavers built. Coffee-glasses steamed in small bars.

In the big glass-paned house, still dripping with water, the children in mourning stared at the marvellous images.

A door slammed, and on the village square, the boy swung his arms, in complicity with the weathervanes and steeplecocks all about him, under the sparkle of a sudden downpour.

Madame *** installed a piano in the Alps. Mass and first communion were celebrated at the hundred thousand altars in the cathedral.

The caravans set off. And the Hôtel Splendide was erected in the icy chaos of the polar night.

From that time on, the Moon could hear jackals howling through deserts of thyme, – and clod-hopping idylls grumbling in the orchard. Next, in the violet clump of leafing trees, Eucharis told me it was spring.[1]

– Surge up, pond, – Foam, roll over the bridge, and over the woods; – black palls and organs, – thunder and lightning; – rise and roll above us; – waters and sorrows, rise and bring back the Floods.

For since they went away, – ah, the precious gems burying themselves, and the opened flowers! – life weighs heavy! and the Queen, the Witch who lights her fire in an earthen cauldron, will never consent to tell us what she knows, and what we do not.

ENFANCE

I

Cette idole, yeux noirs et crin jaune, sans parents ni cour, plus noble que la fable, mexicaine et flamande; son domaine, azur et verdure insolents, court sur des plages nommées, par des vagues sans vaisseaux, de noms férocement grecs, slaves, celtiques.

A la lisière de la forêt – les fleurs de rêve tintent, éclatent, éclairent, – la fille á lèvre d'orange, les genoux croisés dans le clair déluge qui sourd des prés, nudité qu'ombrent, traversent et habillent les arcs-en-ciel, la flore, la mer.

Dames qui tournoient sur les terrasses voisines de la mer; enfantes et géantes, superbes noires dans la mousse vert-de-gris, bijoux debout sur le sol gras des bosquets et des jardinets dégelés – jeunes mères et grandes sœurs aux regards pleins de pèlerinages, sultanes, princesses de démarche et de costume tyranniques, petites étrangères et personnes doucement malheureuses.

Quel ennui, l'heure du «cher corps» et «cher cœur».

II

C'est elle, la petite morte, derrière les rosiers. – La jeune maman trépassée descend le perron – La calèche du cousin crie sur le sable – Le petit frère – (il est aux Indes!) là, devant le couchant, sur le pré d'œillets. – Les vieux qu'on a enterrés tout droits dans le rempart aux giroflées.

L'essaim des feuilles d'or entoure la maison du général. Ils sont dans le midi. On suit la route rouge pour arriver à l'auberge vide. Le château est à vendre; les persiennes sont détachées. – Le curé aura emporté la clef de l'église. – Autour du parc, les loges des gardes sont inhabitées. Les palissades sont si hautes qu'on ne voit que les cimes bruissantes. D'ailleurs il n'y a rien à voir là-dedans.

CHILDHOOD

I

This idol, dark-eyed with a yellow shock of hair, without kin or court, nobler than fables, Mexican and Flemish; inhabiting a domain of insolent azure and green that runs over beaches to which waves with no ships give fierce names, Greek, Slav, Celtic.

At the edge of the woods – the dream flowers tinkle, burst, flare, – the girl with orange lips, her knees crossed in the clear flood that surges from the meadows, nakedness shaded, traversed and clothed by the rainbows, flora, the sea.

Ladies strolling on the terraces by the sea; little girls and giantesses, imposing black women in the grey-green moss, jewels standing on the fertile soil of the thawed groves and small gardens – young mothers and elder sisters with eyes haunted by pilgrimage, the wives of sultans, princesses with tyrannical bearing and dress, little foreign girls and demurely sorrowful figures.

How tiresome it is, the moment of caresses and endearments.

II

There she is, the little dead girl, behind the rose bushes. – The young mamma, deceased, is coming down the steps – The cousin's carriage scrunches on the sand – Over there stands the young brother – (he is in the Colonies!), silhouetted against the setting sun, over the meadow of pinks. – The old people they have buried are standing there in the wallflower rampart.

The swarm of golden leaves surrounds the general's house. These people live in the Midi. – You take the red road to get to the deserted inn. The country mansion is up for sale; the shutters hang loose. – The priest must have removed the key to the church. – The keepers' lodges around the park grounds are no longer lived in. The fences are so high that you can only see the rustling tree tops. Besides, there is nothing to see in there.

Les prés remontent aux hameaux sans coqs, sans enclumes.
L'écluse est levée. O les calvaires et les moulins du désert, les
îles et les meules.

Des fleurs magiques bourdonnaient. Les talus *le* berçaient. Des
bêtes d'une élégance fabuleuse circulaient. Les nuées s'amas-
saient sur la haute mer faite d'une éternité de chaudes larmes.

III

Au bois il y a un oiseau, son chant vous arrête et vois fait rougir.
Il y a une horloge qui ne sonne pas.
Il y a une fondrière avec un nid de bêtes blanches.
Il y a une cathédrale qui descend et un lac qui monte.
Il y a une petite voiture abandonnée dans le taillis, ou qui
descend le sentier en courant, enrubannée.
Il y a une troupe de petits comédiens en costumes, aperçus
sur la route à travers la lisière du bois.
Il y a enfin, quand l'on a faim et soif, quelqu'un qui vous
chasse.

IV

Je suis le saint, en prière sur la terrasse, – comme les bêtes
pacifiques paissent jusqu'à la mer de Palestine.
Je suis le savant au fauteuil sombre. Les branches et la pluie
se jettent à la croisée de la bibliothèque.
Je suis le piéton de la grand'route par les bois nains; la rumeur
des écluses couvre mes pas. Je vois longtemps la mélancolique
lessive d'or du couchant.
Je serais bien l'enfant abandonné sur la jetée partie à la
haute mer, le petit valet suivant l'allée dont le front touche le
ciel.
Les sentiers son âpres. Les monticules se couvrent de genêts.
L'air est immobile. Que les oiseaux et les sources sont loin! Ce
ne peut être que la fin du monde, en avançant.

V

Qu'on me loue enfin ce tombeau, blanchi à la chaux avec les
lignes du ciment en relief – très loin sous terre.

The fields slope up to small villages with no cockerels, no anvils. The sluice gate is up. Ah, the Calvaries and windmills of the wastes, the islands and the haystacks.

Magic flowers were droning. The slopes cradled *him*. Fabulously sleek animals wandered about. The clouds were gathering over the open sea, that eternity of warm tears.

III

In the wood there is a bird, its song makes you stop and blush.
There is a clock that never strikes.
There is a hole in the ground with a nest of white animals.
There is a cathedral that plunges down and a lake that rises up.
There is a small cart left there in the copse, or which runs down the track with its ribbons flying.
There is a troupe of little actors in costume, glimpsed on the road through the outskirts of the wood.
And then, when you feel hungry and thirsty, there is someone who chases you away.

IV

I am the saint, at prayer on the terrace, – as the docile beasts graze down to the Sea of Palestine.
I am the scholar in his dark armchair. The branches and the rain thrash against the library window.
I am the traveller walking the high road through the stunted woods; the roar from sluice gates drowns my footsteps. For a long while I can see the melancholy gold wash of the sunset.
I could well be the child abandoned on the jetty washed far out to sea, the little farm boy following the lane which crests up to the sky.
The paths are rough. The mounds are covered with broom. The air is still. How distant now the birds and the water! It can only be the end of the world, there ahead.

V

In the end let them rent me this tomb, whitewashed and with the lines of the cement in relief – far down beneath the ground.

Je m'accoude à la table, la lampe éclaire très vivement ces - journaux que je suis idiot de relire, ces livres sans intérêt.

A une distance énorme au-dessus de mon salon souterrain, les maisons s'implantent, les brumes s'assemblent. La boue est rouge ou noire. Ville monstrueuse, nuit sans fin!

Moins haut, sont des égouts. Aux côtés, rien que l'épaisseur du globe. Peut-être les gouffres d'azur, des puits de feu. C'est peut-être sur ces plans que se rencontrent lunes et comètes, mers et fables.

Aux heures d'amertume je m'imagine des boules de saphir, de métal. Je suis maître du silence. Pourquoi une apparence de soupirail blêmirait-elle au coin de la voûte?

I lean my elbows on the table, the lamp casts the brightest light on the newspapers I am fool enough to reread, on these books devoid of interest.

At an enormous distance above my underground living-room, houses put down roots, mists gather. The mud is red or black. Monstrous city, endless night!

Less high above me are sewers. Around me, only the density of the globe. Chasms of azure perhaps, wells of fire. These are perhaps the planes on which moons and comets, oceans and fables meet.

In my bitter hours, I imagine balls of sapphire, of metal. I am a master of the silence. Why is it that something like a light shaft seems to gleam palely at the corner of the vaulted ceiling?

CONTE

Un Prince était vexé de ne s'être employé jamais qu'à la perfection des générosités vulgaires. Il prévoyait d'étonnantes révolutions de l'amour, et soupçonnait ses femmes de pouvoir mieux que cette complaisance agrémentée de ciel et de luxe. Il voulait voir la vérité, l'heure du désir et de la satisfaction essentiels. Que ce fût ou non une aberration de piété, il voulut. Il possédait au moins un assez large pouvoir humain.

Toutes les femmes qui l'avaient connu furent assassinées. Quel saccage du jardin de la beauté! Sous le sabre, elles le bénirent. Il n'en commanda point de nouvelles. – Les femmes réapparurent.

Il tua tous ceux qui le suivaient, après la chasse ou les libations. – Tous le suivaient.

Il s'amusa à égorger les bêtes de luxe. Il fit flamber les palais. Il se ruait sur les gens et les taillait en pièces. – La foule, les toits d'or, les belles bêtes existaient encore.

Peut-on s'extasier dans la destruction, se rajeunir par la cruauté! Le peuple ne murmura pas. Personne n'offrit le concours de ses vues.

Un soir il galopait fièrement. Un Génie apparut, d'une beauté ineffable, inavouable même. De sa physionomie et de son maintien ressortait la promesse d'un amour multiple et complexe! d'un bonheur indicible, insupportable même! Le Prince et le Génie s'anéantirent probablement dans la santé essentielle. Comment n'auraient-ils pas pu en mourir? Ensemble donc ils moururent.

Mais ce Prince décéda, dans son palais, à un âge ordinaire. Le prince était le Génie. Le Génie était le Prince.

La musique savante manque à notre désir.

TALE

A Prince was vexed because he had only ever spent his time excelling in the most humdrum acts of generosity. He used to foresee amazing revolutions of love, and suspected his wives of being capable of better things than their usual compliance enhanced by heaven and by luxury. He wanted to see the truth, the moment of essential desire and gratification. Whether or not this was an aberration of piety, this is what he wanted. His worldly power was great enough at least.

Every woman he had known was put to death. What mayhem in the garden of beauty! At sword point, they poured blessings on him. He gave orders for no more women. – The women reappeared.

He killed all those who followed him, after hunting-parties or drinking-feasts. – They all went on following him.

He derived pleasure from slaughtering exotic animals. He set fire to palaces. He hurled himself at people and hacked them to pieces. – The people, the golden rooftops, the rare beasts continued to exist.

Is it possible to find ecstasy in destruction, to rejuvenate oneself through cruelty! There was no murmur from the people. No one offered to support his ideas.

One evening, he was galloping along proudly. A Genie appeared, of indescribable beauty, impossible even to admit. His features and bearing offered the promise of a multiple and complex love! of unspeakable, even unbearable happiness! In all likelihood, the Prince and the Genie annihilated each other and merged into essential health. How could they have not died from it? Together, then, they died.

Yet this Prince died, in his palace, at a normal age. The Prince was the Genie. The Genie was the Prince.

No skill of music can equal our desire.

PARADE

Des drôles très solides. Plusieurs ont exploité vos mondes. Sans besoins et peu pressés de mettre en œuvre leurs brillantes facultés et leur expérience de vos consciences. Quels hommes mûrs! Des yeux hébétés à la façon de la nuit d'été, rouges et noirs, tricolores, d'acier piqué d'étoiles d'or; des facies déformés, plombés, blêmis, incendiés; des enrouements folâtres! La démarche cruelle des oripeaux! – Il y a quelques jeunes, – comment regarderaient-ils Chérubin? – pourvus de voix effrayantes et de quelques ressources dangereuses. On les envoie prendre du dos en ville, affublés d'un *luxe* dégoûtant.

Ô le plus violent Paradis de la grimace enragée! Pas de comparaison avec vos Fakirs et les autres bouffonneries scéniques. Dans des costumes improvisés avec le goût du mauvais rêve ils jouent des complaintes, des tragédies de malandrins et de demi-dieux spirituels comme l'histoire ou les religions ne l'ont jamais été. Chinois, Hottentots, bohémiens, niais, hyènes, Molochs, vieilles démences, démons sinistres, ils mêlent les tours populaires, maternels, avec les poses et les tendresses bestiales. Ils interpréteraient des pièces nouvelles et des chansons «bonnes filles». Maîtres jongleurs, ils transforment le lieu et les personnes, et usent de la comédie magnétique. Les yeux flambent, le sang chante, les os s'élargissent, les larmes et des filets rouges ruissellent. Leur raillerie ou leur terreur dure une minute, ou des mois entiers.

J'ai seul la clef de cette parade sauvage.

ON SHOW

Some very odd characters here, sturdy fellows. Various people have exploited the worlds you inhabit. No urgency in their comfortable lives drove them to set about using their brilliant gifts and their familiarity with the way you see things. What mature men! Eyes bewildered like the summer night, red and black, tricoloured, steel dotted with golden stars; deformed faces, leaden, ashen, aflame; a slight crazy hoarseness of the voice! The cruel swagger of fake finery! – Some of them are young, – what would Cherubino[2] mean to them? – their voices are terrifying and they have a somewhat unnerving astuteness. They are sent to strut around town, dressed up in revolting *luxury*.

O the most violent Paradise of the maddened clenched-up face! No comparison with your Fakirs or all those other theatrical antics. With their costumes hastily thrown together like something out of a bad dream they act out scenes of lamentation, tragic tales of brigands and of demi-gods, with a zest that history or religions never had. Chinese, Hottentots, gypsies, gawping fools, hyenas, Molochs,[3] ancient lunacies, sinister demons, they mix popular turns, tales-your-mother-told-you, with bestial posturings and endearments. They would be quite ready to put on new plays and sentimental songs. These master jugglers transform place and character, and their acting involves hypnosis. Eyes flare, the blood sings, the bones grow in size, tears and red trickles flow. The jibes and the terror last no time at all, or leave their impact for months on end.

I alone hold the key to this wild spectacle.

ANTIQUE

Gracieux fils de Pan! Autour de ton front couronné de fleurettes et de baies tes yeux, des boules précieuses, remuent. Tachées de lies brunes, tes joues se creusent. Tes crocs luisent. Ta poitrine ressemble à une cithare, des tintements circulent dans tes bras blonds. Ton cœur bat dans ce ventre où dort le double sexe. Promène-toi, la nuit, en mouvant doucement cette cuisse, cette seconde cuisse et cette jambe de gauche.

CLASSICAL

Graceful son of Pan! Around your brow crowned with tiny flowers and berries your eyes, precious globes, are moving. Stained with russet wine-lees, your cheeks have hollow pockets. Your fangs gleam. Your chest is like a cithara, tinkling notes move about your blond arms. Your heart-beat pulses in that belly where the ambiguous sex nestles. Walk in the night, gently moving that thigh, then the other, and that leg, the left one.

BEING BEAUTEOUS

Devant une neige un Être de Beauté de haute taille. Des sifflements de mort et des cercles de musique sourde font monter, s'élargir et trembler comme un spectre ce corps adoré; des blessures écarlates et noires éclatent dans les chairs superbes. Les couleurs propres de la vie se foncent, dansent, et se dégagent autour de la Vision, sur le chantier. Et les frissons s'élèvent et grondent et la saveur forcenée de ces effets se chargeant avec les sifflements mortels et les rauques musiques que le monde, loin derrière nous, lance sur notre mère de beauté, – elle recule, elle se dresse. Oh! nos os sont revêtus d'un nouveau corps amoureux.

———

Ô la face cendrée, l'écusson de crin, les bras de cristal! Le canon sur lequel je dois m'abattre à travers la mêlée des arbres et de l'air léger!

BEING BEAUTEOUS

Against a snowscape a tall Figure of Beauty. Deathly hissing sounds and circles of muffled music cause this beloved body to rise, to expand and quiver like a ghost; scarlet and black wounds burst open in the magnificent naked flesh. The natural colours of life deepen, dance and display themselves around the Vision as it comes into being. And the shudders rise and rumble amid the frenzied flavour of these manifestations as they become heavy with the deadly hiss and the raucous music which the world, left far behind us, hurls at her, our mother of beauty, – she recoils and rears herself up. Oh! our bones are now reclothed with newly desiring bodies.

———

O the ashen face, the horsehair escutcheon, the crystal arms! The cannon I must fall upon through the skirmish of trees and the weightless air!

VIES

I

Ô les énormes avenues du pays saint, les terrasses du temple!
Qu'a-t-on fait du brahmane qui m'expliqua les Proverbes?
D'alors, de là-bas, je vois encore même les vieilles! Je me
souviens des heures d'argent et de soleil vers les fleuves, la main
de la campagne sur mon épaule, et de nos caresses debout dans
les plaines poivrées. – Un envol de pigeons écarlates tonne
autour de ma pensée. – Exilé ici j'ai eu une scène où jouer les
chefs-d'œuvre dramatiques de toutes les littératures. Je vous
indiquerais les richesses inouïes. J'observe l'histoire des trésors
que vous trouvâtes. Je vois la suite! Ma sagesse est aussi
dédaignée que le chaos. Qu'est mon néant, auprès de la stupeur
qui vous attend?

II

Je suis un inventeur bien autrement méritant que tous ceux
qui m'ont précédé; un musicien même, qui ai trouvé quelque
chose comme la clef de l'amour. A présent, gentilhomme d'une
campagne aigre au ciel sobre, j'essaie de m'émouvoir au
souvenir de l'enfance mendiante, de l'apprentissage ou de l'arri-
vée en sabots, des polémiques, des cinq ou six veuvages, et
quelques noces où ma forte tête m'empêcha de monter au
diapason des camarades. Je ne regrette pas ma vieille part de
gaîté divine: l'air sobre de cette aigre campagne alimente fort
activement mon atroce scepticisme. Mais comme ce scepticisme
ne peut désormais être mis en œuvre, et que d'ailleurs je suis
dévoué à un trouble nouveau, – j'attends de devenir un très
méchant fou.

III

Dans un grenier où je fus enfermé à douze ans j'ai connu le
monde, j'ai illustré la comédie humaine. Dans un cellier j'ai

LIVES

I

O the vast avenues of the holy land, the terraces of the temple! What has become of the Brahmin who once explained the Proverbs to me? From that time, from that distant place, I can still see even the old women! I remember hours of silver and sunlight towards the rivers, the landscape with its hand on my shoulder, and our caresses as we stood on the spiced plains. – A soaring flock of scarlet pigeons is thundering around my thoughts. – In exile here, I did once have a stage where I could perform the dramatic masterpieces of all literatures. I would show you the unheard-of riches. I now observe the history of the treasures you once discovered. I can see what is to come! My wisdom is as despised as chaos. What is my nothingness beside the stupor that awaits you?

II

I am an inventor with merits quite distinct from all those who have preceded me; a musician, if you like, who has discovered something akin to the key of love. At present, as a country gentleman in a sour landscape with a sober sky, I am trying to be moved by the memory of a pauper's childhood, of apprenticeship or arrival in wooden shoes, of polemics, of five or six widowhoods, and of several drinking-bouts when a strong head preserved me from the excesses of my drinking-partners. I do not regret my former share of divine gaiety: the sober air of this sour landscape feeds my black scepticism very actively. But since such scepticism can now no longer be put to use, and because I am given over to a new kind of disquiet, – I expect to succumb to a particularly evil state of insanity.

III

In a garret where I was locked up when I was twelve, I came to know the world, I illustrated the human comedy. I learned my

appris l'histoire. A quelque fête de nuit dans une cité du Nord j'ai rencontré toutes les femmes des anciens peintres. Dans un vieux passage à Paris on m'a enseigné les sciences classiques. Dans une magnifique demeure cernée par l'Orient entier j'ai accompli mon immense œuvre et passé mon illustre retraite. J'ai brassé mon sang. Mon devoir m'est remis. Il ne faut même plus songer à cela. Je suis réellement d'outre-tombe, et pas de commissions.

history in a store-cupboard. At some nocturnal festival in a Northern city I met all the women of the early painters. In an old back street in Paris I was taught the classical sciences. In a magnificent dwelling surrounded by the entire Orient I completed my vast work and spent my distinguished retirement. I stirred up my blood. I am exonerated from my duty. I don't even have to think about it any more. I am literally from beyond the grave, and with no obligations.

DÉPART

Assez vu. La vision s'est rencontrée à tous les airs.

Assez eu. Rumeurs des villes, le soir, et au soleil, et toujours.

Assez connu. Les arrêts de la vie. – Ô Rumeurs et Visions!

Départ dans l'affection et le bruit neufs!

DEPARTURE

Enough seen. The vision was encountered in all appearances.

Enough experienced. The rumbling sounds of cities, in the evening, and in sunlight, and for ever.

Enough known. The points of standstill in life. – Rumblings and Visions!

Departure into new affection and new sound!

ROYAUTÉ

Un beau matin, chez un peuple fort doux, un homme et une femme superbes criaient sur la place publique.«Mes amis, je veux qu'elle soit reine!» «Je veux être reine!» Elle riait et tremblait. Il parlait aux amis de révélation, d'épreuve terminée. Ils se pâmaient l'un contre l'autre.

En effet ils furent rois toute une matinée où les tentures carminées se relevèrent sur les maisons, et toute l'après-midi, où ils s'avancèrent du côté des jardins de palmes.

ROYALTY

One fine morning, in a land of very gentle people, a magnificent man and woman were shouting out for all to hear: 'My friends, I want her to be queen!' 'I want to be queen!' She was laughing and shaking. He was speaking to their friends about revelation, about an ordeal that was over. They were swooning against each other.

And they *were* monarchs for a whole morning, during which crimson hangings were hoisted on the house fronts, and for the whole afternoon, when they made their way towards gardens of palm trees.

A UNE RAISON

Un coup de ton doigt sur le tambour décharge tous les sons et commence la nouvelle harmonie.

Un pas de toi. C'est la levée des nouveaux hommes et leur enmarche.

Ta tête se détourne: le nouvel amour! Ta tête se retourne, – le nouvel amour!

«Change nos lots, crible les fléaux, à commencer par le temps», te chantent ces enfants. «Élève n'importe où la substance de nos fortunes et de nos vœux» on t'en prie.

Arrivée de toujours, qui t'en iras partout.

TO A REASON

One tap of your finger on the drum releases every sound and begins the new harmony.

You take one step. A new race of men is levied and marches forth.

You turn your head away: new love! You look back again, – new love!

'Change our lot, destroy the plagues, and first of all the plague of time', these children chant to you. 'Give more substance to our fortunes and our desires, no matter where', they beg you.

You arrived here from forever, you will leave for everywhere.

MATINÉE D'IVRESSE

Ô *mon* Bien! ô *mon* Beau! Fanfare atroce où je ne trébuche point! chevalet féerique! Hourra pour l'œuvre inouïe et pour le corps merveilleux, pour la première fois! Cela commença sous les rires des enfants, cela finira par eux. Ce poison va rester dans toutes nos veines même quand, la fanfare tournant, nous serons rendu à l'ancienne inharmonie. Ô maintenant nous si digne de ces tortures! rassemblons fervemment cette promesse surhumaine faite à notre corps et à notre âme créés: cette promesse, cette démence! L'élégance, la science, la violence! On nous a promis d'enterrer dans l'ombre l'arbre du bien et du mal, de déporter les honnêtetés tyranniques, afin que nous amenions notre très pur amour. Cela commença par quelques dégoûts et cela finit, – ne pouvant nous saisir sur-le-champ de cette éternité, – cela finit par une débandade de parfums.

Rire des enfants, discrétion des esclaves, austérité des vierges, horreur des figures et des objets d'ici, sacrés soyez-vous par le souvenir de cette veille. Cela commençait par toute la rustrerie, voici que cela finit par des anges de flamme et de glace.

Petite veille d'ivresse, sainte! quand ce ne serait que pour le masque dont tu nous as gratifié. Nous t'affirmons, méthode! Nous n'oublions pas que tu as glorifié hier chacun de nos âges. Nous avons foi au poison. Nous savons donner notre vie tout entière tous les jours.

Voici le temps des *Assassins*.

MORNING OF DRUNKEN ECSTASY

Oh *my* Good! *my* Beauty! Hideous fanfare in which I do not falter! magical easel of torture! Hurrah for the unheard-of work and the wondrous body, for the first time! It began amid children's laughter, it will end there. This poison will remain in all our veins even when the fanfare sours and returns us to former disharmony. But let us now, we so deserving of this torture, fervently muster the superhuman promise made to our created bodies and souls: that promise, that insanity. Refinement, knowledge, violence! We have been promised that the tree of good and evil shall be buried in darkness, that tyrannical proprieties shall be exiled, so that we can usher in the uncontaminated perfection of our love. It began with a certain disgust and it ended, – since we are unable to seize hold of this eternity here and now, – it ended in a riot of perfumes.

Children's laughter, discreet attention of slaves, austerity of virgins, horror of the faces and objects in this place, may you be hallowed by the memory of this vigil. It began in utter crudity, and now it ends in angels of fire and ice.

Little drunken vigil, holy! if only for the mask with which you have honoured us. Method, we assert you! We do not forget that yesterday you glorified every stage of our lives. We have faith in the poison. We know how to give our whole life each day.

This is the time of the *Assassins*.[4]

PHRASES

Quand le monde sera réduit en un seul bois noir pour nos quatre yeux étonnés, – en une plage pour deux enfants fidèles, – en une maison musicale pour notre claire sympathie, – je vous trouverai.

Qu'il n'y ait ici-bas qu'un vieillard seul, calme et beau, entouré d'un «luxe inouï», – et je suis à vos genoux.

Que j'aie réalisé tous vos souvenirs, – que je sois celle qui sait vous garrotter, – je vous étoufferai.

Quand nous sommes très forts, – qui recule? très gais, qui tombe de ridicule? Quand nous sommes très-méchants, que ferait-on de nous.

Parez-vous, dansez, riez, – Je ne pourrai jamais envoyer l'Amour par la fenêtre.

– Ma camarade, mendiante, enfant monstre! comme ça t'est égal, ces malheureuses et ces manœuvres, et mes embarras. Attache-toi à nous avec ta voix impossible, ta voix! unique flatteur de ce vil désespoir.

PHRASES

When the world has been scaled down to one single dark wood for our four astonished eyes, – to a beach for two inseparable children, – to a musical house for our untroubled sympathy, – I shall find you.

Let there be a single old man left on earth, calm and handsome, surrounded by 'untold wealth', – and I shall be at your feet.

Let me have realized all your memories, – let me be the woman who can bind you hand and foot, – I shall suffocate you.

———

When we are very strong, – who draws back? very gay, who collapses in ridicule? When we are very evil, what would they do to us?

Adorn yourself, dance, laugh, – I shall never be able to send Love out of the window.

———

– My companion, beggar-girl, monster child! how little you care about these unhappy women and these manoeuvres, and my difficulties. Attach yourself to us with your impossible voice, your voice! the sole redeeming feature of this vile despair.

[PHRASES]

Une matinée couverte, en Juillet. Un goût de cendres vole dans l'air; – une odeur de bois suant dans l'âtre, – les fleurs rouies – le saccage des promenades – la bruine des canaux par les champs – pourquoi pas déjà les joujoux et l'encens?

————

J'ai tendu des cordes de clocher à clocher; des guirlandes de fenêtre à fenêtre; des chaînes d'or d'étoile à étoile, et je danse.

————

Le haut étang fume continuellement. Quelle sorcière va se dresser sur le couchant blanc? quelles violettes frondaisons vont descendre?

————

Pendant que les fonds publics s'écoulent en fêtes de fraternité, il sonne une cloche de feu rose dans les nuages.

————

Avivant un agréable goût d'encre de Chine une poudre noire pleut doucement sur ma veillée, – Je baisse les feux du lustre, je me jette sur le lit, et tourné du côté de l'ombre je vous vois, mes filles! mes reines!

[PHRASES]

An overcast morning, in July. A taste of ashes floats through the air; – a smell of wood sweltering in the fireplace, – the retted flowers – the devastated walks – the drizzle of canals across the fields – why not toys and incense this early?

———

I have hung ropes from steeple to steeple; garlands from window to window; golden chains from star to star, and I am dancing.

———

The upland pond is always steaming. What witch is going to loom up against the white sunset? what violet foliage is going to fall?

———

While public money is being poured out in celebrations of brotherhood, a bell of rose-coloured fire rings in the clouds.

———

Heightening a pleasant flavour of Indian ink, a black powder falls like gentle rain on my vigil, – I turn down the gas lamp, throw myself on the bed, and as I turn towards the shadow, I can see you, my young girls! my queens!

OUVRIERS

Ô cette chaude matinée de février. Le Sud inopportun vint relever nos souvenirs d'indigents absurdes, notre jeune misère.

Henrika avait une jupe de coton à carreau blanc et brun, qui a dû être portée au siècle dernier, un bonnet à rubans, et un foulard de soie. C'était bien plus triste qu'un deuil. Nous faisions un tour dans la banlieue. Le temps était couvert et ce vent du Sud excitait toutes les vilaines odeurs des jardins ravagés et des prés desséchés.

Cela ne devait pas fatiguer ma femme au même point que moi. Dans une flache laissée par l'inondation du mois précédent à un sentier assez haut elle me fit remarquer de très petits poissons.

La ville, avec sa fumée et ses bruits de métiers, nous suivait très loin dans les chemins. Ô l'autre monde, l'habitation bénie par le ciel et les ombrages! Le sud me rappelait les misérables incidents de mon enfance, mes désespoirs d'été, l'horrible quantité de force et de science que le sort a toujours éloignée de moi. Non! nous ne passerons pas l'été dans cet avare pays où nous ne serons jamais que des orphelins fiancés. Je veux que ce bras durci ne traîne plus *une chère image*.

WORKERS

The warmth of that February morning! The unseasonable South wind came and revived the memories of the absurd poverty-stricken people we are, the misery of our young lives.

Henrika was wearing a brown-and-white checked cotton skirt, the kind of thing that must have been worn in the last century, a bonnet with ribbons, and a silk head-scarf. It was more dismal than a funeral procession. We were taking a stroll in the outskirts of the city. The sky was overcast and that South wind stirred up all the filthy smells from the ravaged gardens and the parched fields.

It cannot have been as much of a strain for my wife as it was for me. In a pool of water left by the floods of the previous month on a fairly high path she drew my attention to some tiny fish.

The city, with its smoke and the noise of its factories, followed us a long way on our walk. Oh the other world, the dwelling-place blessed by the sky and the shadowy trees! The South wind brought back to mind the miserable incidents of my childhood, my despairs in summer, the appalling amount of strength and knowledge fate has always kept away from me. No! we shall not spend the summer in this miserly part of the world where we shall never be anything but betrothed waifs. I want this hardened arm to stop dragging along *a cherished dream.*

LES PONTS

Des ciels gris de cristal. Un bizarre dessin de ponts, ceux-ci droits, ceux-là bombés, d'autres descendant ou obliquant en angles sur les premiers, et ces figures se renouvelant dans les autres circuits éclairés du canal, mais tous tellement longs et légers que les rives chargées de dômes s'abaissent et s'amoindrissent. Quelques-uns de ces ponts sont encore chargés de masures. D'autres soutiennent des mâts, des signaux, de frêles parapets. Des accords mineurs se croisent, et filent, des cordes montent des berges. On distingue une veste rouge, peut-être d'autres costumes et des instruments de musique. Sont-ce des airs populaires, des bouts de concerts seigneuriaux, des restants d'hymnes publics? L'eau est grise et bleue, large comme un bras de mer. – Un rayon blanc, tombant du haut du ciel, anéantit cette comédie.

THE BRIDGES

Grey crystal skies. A strange pattern of bridges, some straight, some curved, others sloping down or cutting across the first at an angle, and these figures recurring in the other lamp-lit stretches of the canal, but each bridge so long and light that the dome-laden banks sink and diminish in size. Some of these bridges are still covered with small hovels. Others support masts, signals, flimsy parapets. Minor chords cross over, and sustain their sound, cord ropes rise up from the banks. I can make out a red jacket, perhaps other costumes and musical instruments. Are these popular songs, snatches of concerts from the castle, the remnants of public anthems? The water is grey and blue, wide as an inlet of the sea. – A ray of white light, falling from high in the sky, obliterates this sham scene.

VILLE

Je suis un éphémère et point trop mécontent citoyen d'une métropole crue moderne parce que tout goût connu a été éludé dans les ameublements et l'extérieur des maisons aussi bien que dans le plan de la ville. Ici vous ne signaleriez les traces d'aucun monument de superstition. La morale et la langue sont réduites à leur plus simple expression, enfin! Ces millions de gens qui n'ont pas besoin de se connaître amènent si pareillement l'éducation, le métier et la vieillesse, que ce cours de vie doit être plusieurs fois moins long que ce qu'une statistique folle trouve pour les peuples du continent. Aussi comme, de ma fenêtre, je vois des spectres nouveaux roulant à travers l'épaisse et éternelle fumée de charbon, – notre ombre des bois, notre nuit d'été! – des Erinnyes nouvelles, devant mon cottage qui est ma patrie et tout mon cœur puisque tout ici ressemble à ceci, – la Mort sans pleurs, notre active fille et servante, un Amour désespéré, et un joli Crime piaulant dans la boue de la rue.

CITY

I am an ephemeral and by no means over-discontented citizen of a metropolis considered to be modern because all recognized sense of taste has been avoided in the furnishings and the exteriors of its houses as well as in the city planning. You will find no trace here of any monument to superstitious belief. In short, morals and language have been reduced to their simplest form of expression! The millions of people who have no need to know one another conduct their education, their work and their old age in such a uniform manner that their life-span must be several times shorter than the one that an insane set of statistics attributes to people on the continent. And so it is that, from my window, I can see new spectres rolling through the dense and endless coal smoke, – our woodland shade, our summer night – modern Erinnyes,⁵ in front of this cottage which is my homeland and my whole heart since everything here looks like this, – dry-eyed Death, our diligent daughter and servant, a hopeless Love, and a nice little Crime whimpering away in the filth of the street.

ORNIÈRES

A droite l'aube d'été éveille les feuilles et les vapeurs et les bruits de ce coin du parc, et les talus de gauche tiennent dans leur ombre violette les mille rapides ornières de la route humide. Défilé de féeries. En effet: des chars chargés d'animaux de bois doré, de mâts et de toiles bariolées, au grand galop de vingt chevaux de cirque tachetés, et les enfants et les hommes sur leurs bêtes les plus étonnantes; – vingt véhicules, bossés, pavoisés et fleuris comme des carrosses anciens ou de contes, pleins d'enfants attifés pour une pastorale suburbaine; – Même des cercueils sous leur dais de nuit dressant les panaches d'ébène, filant au trot des grandes juments bleues et noires.

RUTS

To the right the summer dawn awakens the leaves and the mists and the sounds of this corner of the park, and the slopes to the left hold their violet shadow over the thousand rapid ruts on the wet road. A procession of enchantments. It was like this: carts laden with gilded wooden animals, poles and brightly striped canvas, the full gallop of twenty dappled circus horses, both children and men on the most amazing beasts; – twenty wagons, studded, hung with flags and painted with flowers like old coaches or ones out of fairy-tales, full of children dressed up for a suburban idyll; – Even coffins under their canopy of night raising their ebony plumes, moving past to the trot of the great blue-black mares.

VILLES

[I]

L'acropole officielle outre les conceptions de la barbarie moderne les plus coiossales. Impossible d'exprimer le jour mat produit par le ciel immuablement gris, l'éclat impérial des bâtisses, et la neige éternelle du sol. On a reproduit dans un goût d'énormité singulier toutes les merveilles classiques de l'architecture. J'assiste à des expositions de peinture dans des locaux vingt fois plus vastes qu'Hampton-Court. Quelle peinture! Un Nabuchodonosor norwégien a fait construire les escaliers des ministères; les subalternes que j'ai pu voir sont déjà plus fiers que des Brahmas et j'ai tremblé à l'aspect des gardiens de colosses et officiers de constructions. Par le groupement des bâtiments en squares, cours et terrasses fermées, on a évincé les cochers. Les parcs représentent la nature primitive travaillée par un art superbe. Le haut quartier a des parties inexplicables: un bras de mer, sans bateaux, roule sa nappe de grésil bleu entre des quais chargés de candélabres géants. Un pont court conduit à une poterne immédiatement sous le dôme de la Sainte-Chapelle. Ce dôme est une armature d'acier artistique de quinze mille pieds de diamètre environ.

Sur quelques points des passerelles de cuivre, des plates-formes, des escaliers qui contournent les halles et les piliers, j'ai cru pouvoir juger la profondeur de la ville! C'est le prodige dont je n'ai pu me rendre compte: quels sont les niveaux des autres quartiers sur ou sous l'acropole? Pour l'étranger de notre temps la reconnaissance est impossible. Le quartier commerçant est un circus d'un seul style, avec galeries à arcades. On ne voit pas de boutiques. Mais la neige de la chaussée est écrasée; quelques nababs aussi rares que les promeneurs d'un matin de dimanche à Londres, se dirigent vers une diligence de diamants. Quelques divans de velours rouge: on sert des boissons polaires dont le prix varie de huit cents à huit mille roupies. A l'idée de chercher des théâtres sur ce circus, je me réponds que les boutiques doivent contenir des drames assez sombres. Je pense qu'il y a

CITIES

[1]

The official acropolis outdoes the most colossal conceptions of modern barbarity. There is no way to describe the dull light produced by the unchanging grey sky, the imperial glare of the buildings, and the eternal snow on the ground. They have reconstructed, in singularly outlandish taste, all the wonders of classical architecture. I attend exhibitions of painting in places twenty times the size of Hampton Court. What paintings! A Norwegian Nebuchadnezzar[6] has had the staircases of the ministries built; the minor officials I did see are themselves prouder than [Brahmins][7] and the looks of the guards in front of colossi and of the building officials set me trembling. By grouping the buildings into squares, courtyards and closed-off terraces, they have ousted the cab drivers. The parks are examples of primitive nature worked upon with marvellous art. The better parts of town have inexplicable features; an arm of the sea, without ships, rolls out its sheet of fine blue hail between quays laden with giant candelabra. A short bridge leads to a postern gate right beneath the dome of the Sainte-Chapelle.[8] This dome is an armature of wrought steel approximately fifteen thousand feet in diameter.

At certain points on the copper footbridges, the platforms, the staircases that wind round the covered markets and the pillars, I thought I could gauge the depth of the city! This prodigy eludes me: how far below or above the acropolis are the other parts of it? For the stranger of our time it is impossible to get one's bearings. The commercial district is a circus in a uniform style, with arcaded galleries. There are no shops to be seen. Yet the snow on the streets is trampled; the occasional nabob, as rare as a Sunday-morning stroller in London, moves towards a diamond carriage. The occasional red-velvet divan: they serve polar drinks costing from eight hundred to eight thousand rupees. I think of looking for a theatre in this circus but I decide that the shops themselves must contain some pretty dark dramas. I believe there is a police force; but the laws must

une police; mais la loi doit être tellement étrange, que je renonce à me faire une idée des aventuriers d'ici.

Le faubourg aussi élégant qu'une belle rue de Paris est favorisé d'un air de lumière. L'élément démocratique compte quelque cent âmes. Là encore les maisons ne se suivent pas; le faubourg se perd bizarrement dans la campagne, le «Comté» qui remplit l'occident éternel des forêts et des plantations prodigieuses où les gentilshommes sauvages chassent leurs chroniques sous la lumière qu'on a créée.

be so strange that I give up trying to imagine what the local lawbreakers must be like.

The outlying district, as elegant as a fine street in Paris, enjoys an appearance of light. The democratic element numbers some hundred souls. Here again, the houses are not in rows; the suburb fades away oddly into the countryside, the 'County' that fills the endless west with the forests and the huge plantations where a savage nobility hunt down the newspaper columns by artificial light.

VAGABONDS

Pitoyable frère! Que d'atroces veillées je lui dus! «Je ne me saisissais pas fervemment de cette entreprise. Je m'étais joué de son infirmité. Par ma faute nous retournerions en exil, en esclavage.» Il me supposait un guignon et une innocence très bizarres, et il ajoutait des raisons inquiétantes.

Je répondais en ricanant à ce satanique docteur, et finissais par gagner la fenêtre. Je créais, par-delà la campagne traversée par des bandes de musique rare, les fantômes du futur luxe nocturne.

Après cette distraction vaguement hygiénique je m'étendais sur une paillasse. Et, presque chaque nuit, aussitôt endormi, le pauvre frère se levait, la bouche pourrie, les yeux arrachés, – tel qu'il se rêvait! – et me tirait dans la salle en hurlant son songe de chagrin idiot.

J'avais en effet, en toute sincérité d'esprit, pris l'engagement de le rendre à son état primitif de fils du soleil, – et nous errions, nourris du vin des cavernes et du biscuit de la route, moi pressé de trouver le lieu et la formule.

TRAMPS

Pitiful brother! What hideous sleepless nights I owed to him! 'I was not wild to seize upon this venture. I made light of his weakness. It would be my fault if we were to go back into exile and slavery.' He credited me with the strangest ill-luck and innocence, and for disturbing reasons.

I would reply by sneering at this satanic teacher, and end up moving to the window. I was creating, beyond the landscape traversed by bands of exquisite music, the ghosts of the nocturnal luxury that was to come.

After this vaguely hygienic diversion, I would stretch out on a straw mattress. And, almost every night, as soon as I was asleep, my poor brother would get up, with his stinking mouth and his eyes clawed out, – just as he saw himself in his dreams – and drag me into the room, howling his dream of idiot sorrow.

It is true that I had undertaken, in all sincerity of mind, to restore him to his original state as child of the sun, – and we used to wander, nourished on the wine of caverns and the dry bread of travellers, while I was anxiously searching to discover the place and the right words.

VILLES

[11]

Ce cont des villes! C'est un peuple pour qui se sont montés ces Alleghanys et ces Libans de rêve! Des chalets de cristal et de bois qui se meuvent sur des rails et des poulies invisibles. Les vieux cratères ceints de colosses et de palmiers de cuivre rugissent mélodieusement dans les feux. Des fêtes amoureuses sonnent sur les canaux pendus derrière les chalets. La chasse des carillons crie dans les gorges. Des corporations de chanteurs géants accourent dans des vêtements et des oriflammes éclatants comme la lumière des cimes. Sur les plates-formes au milieu des gouffres les Rolands sonnent leur bravoure. Sur les passerelles de l'abîme et les toits des auberges l'ardeur du ciel pavoise les mâts. L'écroulement des apothéoses rejoint les champs des hauteurs où les centauresses séraphiques évoluent parmi les avalanches. Au-dessus du niveau des plus hautes crêtes une mer troublée par la naissance éternelle de Vénus, chargée de flottes orphéoniques et de la rumeur des perles et des conques précieuses, – la mer s'assombrit parfois avec des éclats mortels. Sur les versants des moissons de fleurs grandes comme nos armes et nos coupes, mugissent. Des cortèges de Mabs en robes rousses, opalines, montent des ravines. Là-haut, les pieds dans la cascade et les ronces, les cerfs tètent Diane. Les Bacchantes des banlieues sanglotent et la lune brûle et hurle. Vénus entre dans les cavernes des forgerons et des ermites. Des groupes de beffrois chantent les idées des peuples. Des châteaux bâtis en os sort la musique inconnue. Toutes les légendes évoluent et les élans se ruent dans les bourgs. Le paradis des orages s'effondre. Les sauvages dansent sans cesse la fête de la nuit. Et une heure je suis descendu dans le mouvement d'un boulevard de Bagdad où des compagnies ont chanté la joie du travail nouveau, sous une brise épaisse, circulant sans pouvoir éluder les fabuleux fantômes des monts où l'on a dû se retrouver.

Quels bons bras, quelle belle heure me rendront cette région d'où viennent mes sommeils et mes moindres mouvements?

CITIES

[II]

These are cities! This is a people for whom these dream Alleghanys[9] and these Lebanons have risen from the ground! Chalets of crystal and wood moving on invisible rails and pulleys. The ancient craters circled by colossi and copper palm-trees roar away melodiously in the flames. Festivals of love ring out over canals hanging behind the chalets. The chase of pealing bells cries out in the gorges. Guilds of giant singers come running in robes and with banners dazzling like the light on mountain tops. On the platforms set in the heart of gulfs the Rolands trumpet their valour.[10] On the footbridges of the abyss and the rooftops of the inns the fires of heaven hang flags out on the poles. The collapse of apotheoses regains the hilltop fields where seraphic centauresses move about among the avalanches. Above the highest crests a sea disturbed by the eternal birth of Venus, spread with choral fleets and alive with the murmur of precious pearls and conches, – this sea sometimes darkens over with deadly flashes of brightness. From the hillsides comes the bellowing of harvests of flowers as big as our weapons and our goblets. Processions of Mabs[11] in russet robes, opaline, move up from the ravines. High up, with their feet in the waterfall and the brambles, the deer suckle at the breast of Diana.[12] The Bacchantes[13] of the suburbs are sobbing and the moon burns and howls. Venus visits the caves of blacksmiths and hermits. Groups of bell-towers sing out the ideas of the nations. Unknown music is coming from castles built of bones. All legends are evolving and excitement dashes out into the villages. The paradise of storms is collapsing. The savages dance the celebration of the night in an endless dance. And, in the space of an hour, I have come down into the bustle of a boulevard in Baghdad where gatherings of people have sung the joy of new labour, in a heavy breeze, moving about without being able to avoid the fabulous ghosts of the mountains where they must have met up once more.

What kindly arms, what lucky hour will restore this region to me, the source of my sleeping hours and my slightest impulses?

VEILLÉES

I

C'est le repos éclairé, ni fièvre ni langueur, sur le lit ou sur le pré.

C'est l'ami ni ardent ni faible. L'ami.

C'est l'aimée ni tourmentante ni tourmentée. L'aimée.

L'air et le monde point cherchés. La vie.

– Était-ce donc ceci?

– Et le rêve fraîchit.

II

L'éclairage revient à l'arbre de bâtisse. Des deux extrémités de la salle, décors quelconques, des élévations harmoniques se joignent. La muraille en face du veilleur est une succession psychologique de coupes de frises, de bandes atmosphériques et d'accidences géologiques. – Rêve intense et rapide de groupes sentimentaux avec des êtres de tous les caractères parmi toutes les apparences.

III

Les lampes et les tapis de la veillée font le bruit des vagues, la nuit, le long de la coque et autour du steerage.

La mer de la veillée, telle que les seins d'Amélie.

Les tapisseries, jusqu'à mi-hauteur, des taillis de dentelle, teinte d'émeraude, où se jettent les tourterelles de la veillée.

....

La plaque du foyer noir, de réels soleils des grèves: ah! puits des magies; seule vue d'aurore, cette fois.

VIGILS

I

This is mindful repose, not fever, not languor, on the bed or on the grass.

This is the friend, neither pressing nor undemanding. The friend.

This is the beloved, neither a tormentor nor tormented. The beloved.

Air and the world unsought. Life.

– So this is what it was?

– And the dream grows cold.

II

The light returns to the roof-beam. From the two ends of the room, nondescript scenes, harmonic elevations meet up together. The wall facing the watcher is a psychological sequence of cross-sections of friezes, atmospheric layers and geological strata. – A vivid, rapid dream of sentimental groups with beings of all kinds in every conceivable setting.

III

The lamps and the rugs of the vigil sound like waves, at night, along the hull and around the *entrepont*.

The sea of the vigil, like Amélie's breasts.

The wall-hangings, up to half way, thickets of lace, dyed emerald, where the doves of the vigil dart about.

. . . .

The fireback of the blackened hearth, real suns on seashores: ah! wells of magics; the only glimpse of dawn, this time.

MYSTIQUE

Sur la pente du talus les anges tournent leurs robes de laine dans les herbages d'acier et d'émeraude.

Des prés de flammes bondissent jusqu'au sommet du mamelon. A gauche le terreau de l'arête est piétiné par tous les homicides et toutes les batailles, et tous les bruits désastreux filent leur courbe. Derrière l'arête de droite la ligne des orients, des progrès.

Et tandis que la bande en haut du tableau est formée de la rumeur tournante et bondissante des conques des mers et des nuits humaines,

La douceur fleurie des étoiles et du ciel et du reste descend en face du talus, comme un panier, contre notre face, et fait l'abîme fleurant et bleu là-dessous.

MYSTICAL

On the slope of the bank angels turn their woollen robes in pastures of steel and emerald.

Meadows of flame leap up to the top of the knoll. To the left the leaf-mould on the ridge is trampled into the ground by all homicides and all battles, and every sound of disaster pursues its curving path. Behind the ridge on the right, the line of orients, of progress.

And whereas the strip at the top of the picture is formed by the whirling, leaping murmur of conch shells and human nights,

The flowery softness of the stars and the sky and everything else descends opposite the slope, like a basket, against our face, and creates the flowering blue abyss beneath.

AUBE

J'ai embrassé l'aube d'été.

Rien ne bougeait encore au front des palais. L'eau était morte. Les camps d'ombres ne quittaient pas la route du bois. J'ai marché, réveillant les haleines vives et tièdes, et les pierreries regardèrent, et les ailes se levèrent sans bruit.

La première entreprise fut, dans le sentier déjà empli de frais et blêmes éclats, une fleur qui me dit son nom.

Je ris au wasserfall blond qui s'échevela à travers les sapins: à la cime argentée je reconnus la déesse.

Alors je levai un à un les voiles. Dans l'allée, en agitant les bras. Par la plaine, où je l'ai dénoncée au coq. A la grand'ville elle fuyait parmi les clochers et les dômes, et courant comme un mendiant sur les quais de marbre, je la chassais.

En haut de la route, près d'un bois de lauriers, je l'ai entourée avec ses voiles amassés, et j'ai senti un peu son immense corps. L'aube et l'enfant tombèrent au bas du bois.

Au réveil il était midi.

DAWN

I have kissed the summer dawn.

Nothing was yet stirring on the brows of the palaces. The water lay dead. The camps of shadows remained pitched on the road through the woods. I walked, awakening warm living breaths, and the precious stones stared, the wings rose noiselessly.

The first venture, along the path already filled with cool pale glints, was a flower which told me its name.

I laughed at the blonde wasserfall[14] dishevelling its hair among the fir-trees: on the silvered ledge I recognized the goddess.

Then one by one I lifted the veils. Along the pathway, waving my arms. Out on open ground where I denounced her to the cockerel. In the city she fled among the belfries and the domes, and running like a beggar over the marble quays, I chased after her.

At the top of the road, near a laurel grove, I threw my arms around her with her gathered veils and felt something of her immense body. Dawn and the child fell to the ground at the bottom of the grove.

When I woke it was noon.

FLEURS

D'un gradin d'or, – parmi les cordons de soie, les gazes grises, les velours verts et les disques de cristal qui noircissent comme du bronze au soleil, – je vois la digitale s'ouvrir sur un tapis de filigranes d'argent, d'yeux et de chevelures.

Des pièces d'or jaune semées sur l'agate, des piliers d'acajou supportant un dôme d'émeraudes, des bouquets de satin blanc et de fines verges de rubis entourent la rose d'eau.

Tels qu'un dieu aux énormes yeux bleus et aux formes de neige, la mer et le ciel attirent aux terrasses de marbre la foule des jeunes et fortes roses.

FLOWERS

From a golden tier – among the silk ropes, the grey gauzes, green velvets and the crystal discs darkening to bronze in the sunlight, – I can see the foxglove open on a carpet of silver filigree, eyes and hair.

Golden yellow coins scattered on agate, mahogany pillars supporting a dome of emeralds, bunches of white satin and slender stems of rubies surround the water rose.

Like a god with enormous blue eyes and the shapes of snow, the sea and sky draw to the marble terraces the crowd of roses, young and strong.

NOCTURNE VULGAIRE

Un souffle ouvre des brèches operadiques dans les cloisons, – brouille le pivotement des toits rongés, – disperse les limites des foyers, – éclipse les croisées. – Le long de la vigne, m'étant appuyé du pied à une gargouille, – je suis descendu dans ce carrosse dont l'époque est assez indiquée par les glaces convexes, les panneaux bombés et les sophas contournés – Corbillard de mon sommeil, isolé, maison de berger de ma niaiserie, le véhicule vire sur le gazon de la grande route effacée: et dans un défaut en haut de la glace de droite tournoient les blêmes figures lunaires, feuilles, seins; – Un vert et un bleu très foncés envahissent l'image. Dételage aux environs d'une tache de gravier.

– Ici, va-t-on siffler pour l'orage, et les Sodomes, et les Solymes, – et les bêtes féroces et les armées,

– (Postillon et bêtes de songe reprendront-ils sous les plus suffocantes futaies, pour m'enfoncer jusqu'aux yeux dans la source de soie).

– Et nous envoyer, fouettés à travers les eaux clapotantes et les boissons répandues, rouler sur l'aboi des dogues . . .

– Un souffle disperse les limites du foyer.

TAWDRY NOCTURNE

A single breath opens up operatic breaches in the walls, – blurs the swivelling movement of the eroded rooftops, – disperses the boundaries of hearths, – eclipses the windows. – Down the vine, my foot resting on a gargoyle, – I have climbed into this coach whose period is clear enough from the convex window-panes, bulging panels and over-elaborate upholstery – Hearse of my sleep, alone, shepherd's hut of my simple-mindedness, the vehicle veers round on the grass of the overgrown highway: and in a flaw high on the right-hand window, is the revolving pattern of the pale lunar figures, leaves, breasts; – Deepest green and blue invade the picture. Unharnessing near a patch of gravel.

– Here, we will whistle for storms, for Sodoms,[15] for Solymas,[16] – for wild beasts and armies,

– (Coachmen and dream beasts will move on through the most suffocating thickets, and sink me up to the eyes in the spring of silk).

– And send us, whipped through the splashing water and the spilled drinks, to roll over the barking of bulldogs . . .

– One breath disperses the boundaries of the hearth.

MARINE

Les chars d'argent et de cuivre –
Les proues d'acier et d'argent –
Battent l'écume, –
Soulèvent les souches des ronces.
Les courants de la lande
Et les ornières immenses du reflux
Filent circulairement vers l'est,
Vers les piliers de la forêt, –
Vers les fûts de la jetée,
Dont l'angle est heurté par des tourbillons de lumière.

SEASCAPE

The chariots of silver and copper –
The prows of steel and silver –
Beat the foam, –
Uproot the stumps of the bramble.
The currents of the heath
And the huge ruts of the ebb-tide
Flow off in circles to the east,
Towards the columns of the forest, –
Towards the tree-trunks of the jetty,
Its corner buffeted by whirlwinds of light.

FÊTE D'HIVER

La cascade sonne derrière les huttes d'opéra-comique. Des girandoles prolongent, dans les vergers et les allées voisins du Méandre, – les verts et les rouges du couchant. Nymphes d'Horace coiffées au Premier Empire, – Rondes Sibériennes, Chinoises de Boucher. –

WINTER FESTIVAL

The waterfall rumbles behind huts from a comic opera. Girandoles, in the orchard and avenues by the Meander,[17] – prolong the greens and the reds of sunset. Nymphs from Horace, their hair dressed in the style of the First Empire, – Round Siberian women, Chinese women out of Boucher.[18] –

ANGOISSE

Se peut-il qu'Elle me fasse pardonner les ambitions contin-
uellement écrasées, – qu'une fin aisée répare les âges d'indigence,
– qu'un jour de succès nous endorme sur la honte de notre
inhabileté fatale,

(Ô palmes! diamant! – Amour! force! – plus haut que toutes
joies et gloires! – de toutes façons, partout, – Démon, dieu –
Jeunesse de cet être-ci; moi!)

Que des accidents de féerie scientifique et des mouvements de
fraternité sociale soient chéris comme restitution progressive de
la franchise première?...

Mais la Vampire qui nous rend gentils commande que nous
nous amusions avec ce qu'elle nous laisse, ou qu'autrement nous
soyons plus drôles.

Rouler aux blessures, par l'air lassant et la mer; aux supplices,
par le silence des eaux et de l'air meurtriers; aux tortures qui
rient, dans leur silence atrocement houleux.

ANGUISH

Is it possible that She might forgive my continually crushed ambitions, – that a comfortable end might make amends for the ages of poverty, – that a day's success nurse us to sleep on the shame of our fatal ineptitude,

(O palms! diamond! – Love! strength! – higher than all joys and glories! – of every kind, everywhere – Demon, god – Youth of the being here present; myself!)

That accidents of scientific magic and movements of social brotherhood might be held dear as the progressive restitution of original freedom?. . .

But the Vampire who makes us behave ourselves commands us to be content with what she leaves us, or else to be more amusing.

To roll upon wounds, through the exhausting air and the sea; on torments, through the silence of the murderous waters and air; on tortures that mock us, in the hideous swell of their silence.

MÉTROPOLITAIN

Du détroit d'indigo aux mers d'Ossian, sur le sable rose et orange qu'a lavé le ciel vineux viennent de monter et de se croiser des boulevards de cristal habités incontinent par de jeunes familles pauvres qui s'alimentent chez les fruitiers. Rien de riche. – La ville!

Du désert de bitume fuient droit en déroute avec les nappes de brumes échelonnées en bandes affreuses au ciel qui se recourbe, se recule et descend, formé de la plus sinistre fumée noire que puisse faire l'Océan en deuil, les casques, les roues, les barques, les croupes. – La bataille!

Lève la tête: le pont de bois, arqué; les derniers potagers de Samarie; ces masques enluminés sous la lanterne fouettée par la nuit froide; l'ondine niaise à la robe bruyante, au bas de la rivière; les crânes lumineux dans les plans de pois – et les autres fantasmagories – la campagne.

Des routes bordées de grilles et de murs, contenant à peine leurs bosquets, et les atroces fleurs qu'on appellerait cœurs et sœurs, Damas damnant de longueur, – possessions de féeriques aristocraties ultra-Rhénanes, Japonaises, Guaranies, propres encore à recevoir la musique des anciens – et il y a des auberges qui pour toujours n'ouvrent déjà plus – il y a des princesses, et si tu n'es pas trop accablé, l'étude des astres – le ciel.

Le matin oú avec Elle, vous vous débattîtes parmi les éclats de neige, les lèvres vertes, les glaces, les drapeaux noirs et les rayons bleus, et les parfums pourpres du soleil des pôles, – ta force.

METROPOLITAN

From the indigo straits to the seas of Ossian,[19] on the pink-and-orange sand that has been washed by the wine of the sky crystal boulevards have just risen and intersected, inhabited here and there by young families of poor people who get their food from the fruiterer's. Nothing rich here. – The city!

From the asphalt wilderness flee in headlong confusion with the swathes of fog spread out in horrible layers in the sky which curves up, recedes and descends, formed by the most sinister black smoke that can be produced by the Ocean in mourning, the helmets, the wheels, the boats, the rumps. – The battle!

Look up: the wooden bridge, arched; the last vegetable plots of Samaria;[20] these masks lit up beneath the lantern lashed by the chill night; the gawping water-nymph with the noisy dress, in the depths of the river; the luminous skulls in the pea-beds – and the other phantasmagoria – the countryside.

Roads bordered by railings and walls, barely containing their clumps of trees, and the hideous flowers you would call hearts and sisters, Damascus damning with tediousness, – the properties of fairy-tale aristocracies from beyond the Rhine, Japanese, Guarani,[21] still fit to receive music of the old school – and there are inns that never open now, nor ever will – there are princesses, and if you are not too overwhelmed, the study of the stars – the sky.

The morning when, in Her company, you struggled together in the sparkling lights of snow, the green lips, the ice, the black flags and the blue beams of light, and the purple scents of the polar sun, – your strength.

BARBARE

Bien après les jours et les saisons, et les êtres et les pays,

Le pavillon en viande saignante sur la soie des mers et des fleurs arctiques; (elles n'existent pas.)

Remis des vieilles fanfares d'héroïsme – qui nous attaquent encore le cœur et la tête – loin des anciens assassins –

Oh! Le pavillon en viande saignante sur la soie des mers et des fleurs arctiques; (elles n'existent pas)

Douceurs!

Les brasiers pleuvant aux rafales de givre, – Douceurs! – les feux à la pluie du vent de diamants jetée par le cœur terrestre éternellement carbonisé pour nous. – Ô monde! –

(Loin des vieilles retraites et des vieilles flammes, qu'on entend, qu'on sent,)

Les brasiers et les écumes. La musique, virement des gouffres et choc des glaçons aux astres.

Ô Douceurs, ô monde, ô musique! Et là, les formes, les sueurs, les chevelures et les yeux, flottant. Et les larmes blanches, bouillantes, – ô douceurs! – et la voix féminine arrivée au fond des volcans et des grottes arctiques.

Le pavillon . . .

BARBARIC

Long after the days and the seasons, and the creatures and the countries,

The pavilion of bloodied meat on the silk of the seas and Arctic flowers; (they do not exist.)

Delivered from the old fanfares of heroism – which still attack our hearts and heads – far from the old assassins –

Oh! The pavilion of bloodied meat on the silk of the seas and Arctic flowers; (they do not exist)

Sweetness!

Blazing flames raining down in squalls of frost, – Sweetness! – the fires in the wind's diamond rain hurled out by the earth's core eternally burnt to ashes for us – O world! –

(Far from the old retreats and the old flames, which can be heard, can be felt,)

Blazing fires and foams. Music, swirling gulfs and the clash of icicles on the stars.

O Sweetness, o world, o music! And there, the shapes, sweats, heads of hair, eyes, floating. And the white tears, boiling, – o sweetness! – and the female voice reaching the depths of the volcanoes and the Arctic caves.

The pavilion . . .

SOLDE

A vendre ce que les Juifs n'ont pas vendu, ce que noblesse ni crime n'ont goûté, ce qu'ignorent l'amour maudit et la probité infernale des masses: ce que le temps ni la science n'ont pas à reconnaître:

Les Voix reconstituées; l'éveil fraternel de toutes les énergies chorales et orchestrales et leurs applications instantanées; l'occasion, unique, de dégager nos sens!

A vendre les Corps sans prix, hors de toute race, de tout monde, de tout sexe, de toute descendance! Les richesses jaillissant à chaque démarche! Solde de diamants sans contrôle!

A vendre l'anarchie pour les masses; la satisfaction irrépressible pour les amateurs supérieurs; la mort atroce pour les fidèles et les amants!

A vendre les habitations et les migrations, sports, féeries et comforts parfaits, et le bruit, le mouvement et l'avenir qu'ils font!

A vendre les applications de calcul et les sauts d'harmonie inouïs. Les trouvailles et les termes non soupçonnés, possession immédiate,

Élan insensé et infini aux splendeurs invisibles, aux délices insensibles, – et ses secrets affolants pour chaque vice – et sa gaîté effrayante pour la foule –

A vendre les Corps, les voix, l'immense opulence inquestionable, ce qu'on ne vendra jamais. Les vendeurs ne sont pas à bout de solde! Les voyageurs n'ont pas à rendre leur commission de si tôt!

CLEARANCE SALE

For sale what the Jews have not sold, what neither nobility nor crime have tasted, what is unknown to accursed love and to the infernal integrity of the masses: what neither time nor learning needs to acknowledge:

The Voices reconstituted; the fraternal awakening of every choral and orchestral energy and their immediate implementation; the opportunity, a unique one, to liberate our senses!

For sale the Bodies beyond price, beyond all race, all world, all sex, all line of descent! Riches gushing out at every turn! Unlimited sale of diamonds!

For sale anarchy for the masses; irrepressible satisfaction for those who appreciate only the best; gruesome death for the faithful and for lovers!

For sale dwelling-places and migrations, sports, perfect magics and comforts, and the noise, the stir and the future they entail!

For sale unheard-of applications of calculation and jumps in harmony. Unsuspected chance discoveries and terms, with immediate possession,

A senseless and infinite impulse towards invisible splendours and imperceptible delights, – and its alarming secrets for every vice – its terrifying gaiety for the crowd –

For sale the Bodies, the voices, the immense unquestionable opulence, things which will never be sold. The vendors have not cleared their stock! The travellers won't have to present their accounts for some time to come!

FAIRY

Pour Hélène se conjurèrent les sèves ornamentales dans les ombres vierges et les clartés impassibles dans le silence astral. L'ardeur de l'été fut confiée à des oiseaux muets et l'indolence requise à une barque de deuils sans prix par des anses d'amours morts et de parfums affaissés.

– Après le moment de l'air des bûcheronnes à la rumeur du torrent sous la ruine des bois, de la sonnerie des bestiaux à l'écho des vals, et des cris des steppes. –

Pour l'enfance d'Hélène frissonnèrent les fourrures et les ombres, – et le sein des pauvres, et les légendes du ciel.

Et ses yeux et sa danse supérieurs encore aux éclats précieux, aux influences froides, au plaisir du décor et de l'heure uniques.

FAIRY

For Helen the ornamental saps conspired in the virgin darkness and the impassive brightness in the astral silence. The summer heat was entrusted to mute birds and the appropriate indolence to a priceless funeral barge by bays of dead loves and spent perfumes.

– After the time of the song of the woodcutter women to the sound of the torrent beneath the ruin of the woods, of the bells of the cattle ringing to the echo of the valleys and of the cries from the steppes. –

For Helen's childhood furs and shadows stirred, – and the breasts of the poor, and the legends of the sky.

And her eyes and her dancing still superior to the priceless brilliance, to the effects of cold, to the pleasure of the special setting and the hour.

JEUNESSE

I

DIMANCHE

Les calculs de côté, l'inévitable descente du ciel, la visite des souvenirs et la séance des rhythmes occupent la demeure, la tête et le monde de l'esprit.

– Un cheval détale sur le turf suburbain, et le long des cultures et des boisements, percé par la peste carbonique. Une misérable femme de drame, quelque part dans le monde, soupire après des abandons improbables. Les desperadoes languissent après l'orage, l'ivresse et les blessures. De petits enfants étouffent des malédictions le long des rivières. –

Reprenons l'étude au bruit de l'œuvre dévorante qui se rassemble et remonte dans les masses.

II

SONNET

Homme de constitution ordinaire, la chair
n'était-elle pas un fruit pendu dans le verger; – ô
journées enfantes! – le corps un trésor à prodiguer; – ô
aimer, le péril ou la force de Psyché? La terre
avait des versants fertiles en princes et en artistes,
et la descendance et la race vous poussaient aux
crimes et aux deuils: le monde votre fortune et votre
péril. Mais à présent, ce labeur comblé; toi, tes calculs,
– toi, tes impatiences – ne sont plus que votre danse et
votre voix, non fixées et point forcées, quoique d'un double
événement d'invention et de succès + une raison,
– en l'humanité fraternelle et discrète par l'univers
sans images; – la force et le droit réfléchissent la
danse et la voix à présent seulement appréciées.

YOUTH

I

SUNDAY

Sums set aside, the inevitable descent from heaven, the visitation of memories and the séance of rhythms invade the house, the head and the world of the mind.

– A horse bolts off on the suburban racecourse, and along fields and stretches of woodland, stricken with the carbonic plague. A wretched woman out of some drama, somewhere in the world, is sighing for improbable surrenders to passion. Desperadoes long for storms, drunkenness and wounds. Little children stifle curses along river banks. –

Time to turn back to our studies and the sound of the consuming work which gathers and rises again among the masses.

II

SONNET

Man of ordinary constitution, was not the flesh
a fruit hanging there in the orchard; – oh
childhood days! – the body a treasure to squander; – oh
loving, the peril or the strength of Psyche?[22] The earth
had slopes fertile in princes and artists,
and descent and race drove us to
crimes and to grief: the world your fortune and your
peril. But now, that labour fulfilled; you, your calculations,
– you, your bouts of impatience – are no more than your dancing and
your voice, not fixed and not forced, although a reason
for a double outcome of inventiveness and success,
– in brotherly and discreet humanity throughout the
imageless universe; – strength and justice reflect
the dancing and the voice that are valued only now.

III

Les voix instructives exilées ... L'ingénuité physique amèrement rassise ... – Adagio – Ah! l'égoïsme infini de l'adolescence, l'optimisme studieux: que le monde était plein de fleurs cet été! Les airs et les formes mourant ... – Un chœur, pour calmer l'impuissance et l'absence! Un chœur de verres, de mélodies nocturnes ... En effet les nerfs vont vite chasser.

IV

Tu en es encore à la tentation d'Antoine. L'ébat du zèle écourté, les tics d'orgueil puéril, l'affaissement et l'effroi.

Mais tu te mettras à ce travail: toutes les possibilités harmoniques et architecturales s'émouvront autour de ton siège. Des êtres parfaits, imprévus, s'offriront à tes expériences. Dans tes environs affluera rêveusement la curiosité d'anciennes foules et de luxes oisifs. Ta mémoire et tes sens ne seront que la nourriture de ton impulsion créatrice. Quant au monde, quand tu sortiras, que sera-t-il devenu? En tout cas, rien des apparences actuelles.

III

TWENTY YEARS OLD

The voices of instruction exiled ... The ingenuousness of the body bitterly called to order ... – Adagio – Ah! the infinite selfishness of adolescence, the studious optimism: how full of flowers was the world that summer! Tunes and shapes fading away ... – A choir, to soothe impotence and absence! A choir of glasses, of nocturnal melodies ... Yes, the nerves will go adrift soon enough.

IV

You have still not moved beyond the temptation of Anthony.[23] The diminished zest of enthusiasm, the grimaces of puerile pride, the exhaustion and the terror.

But you will apply yourself to this work: all harmonic and architectural possibilities will stir about your seat. Perfect, unforeseen beings will offer themselves up to your experiments. Around you will gather, dreamily, the curiosity of ancient crowds and idle luxuries. Your memory and your senses will merely be the food for your creative impulse. And what of the world, when you leave it behind? Certainly it will have nothing in common with the way it appears now.

GUERRE

Enfant, certains ciels ont affiné mon optique: tous les caractères nuancèrent ma physionomie. Les Phénomènes s'émurent. – A présent l'inflexion éternelle des moments et l'infini des mathématiques me chassent par ce monde où je subis tous les succès civils, respecté de l'enfance étrange et des affections énormes. – Je songe à une Guerre, de droit ou de force, de logique bien imprévue.

C'est aussi simple qu'une phrase musicale.

WAR

As a child, certain skies sharpened my vision: every character finely affected my features. Phenomena shifted about. – Now, the endless inflexion of moments and the infinity of mathematics drive me through this world where I experience every civil success, respected by strange children and unbounded affection. – I dream of a War, of justice or of might, of logic quite beyond expectation.

It is as simple as a musical phrase.

PROMONTOIRE

L'aube d'or et la soirée frissonnante trouvent notre brick en large en face de cette Villa et de ses dépendances, qui forment un promontoire aussi étendu que l'Épire et le Péloponnèse ou que la grand île du Japon, ou que l'Arabie! Des fanums qu'éclaire la rentrée des théories, d'immenses vues de la défense des côtes modernes; des dunes illustrées de chaudes fleurs et de bacchanales; de grands canaux de Carthage et des Embankments d'une Venise louche; de molles éruptions d'Etnas et des crevasses de fleurs et d'eaux des glaciers; des lavoirs entourés de peupliers d'Allemagne; des talus de parcs singuliers penchant des têtes d'Arbres du Japon; les façades circulaires des «Royal» ou des «Grand» de Scarbro' ou de Brooklyn; et leurs railways flanquent, creusent, surplombent les dispositions de cet Hôtel, choisies dans l'histoire des plus élégantes et des plus colossales constructions de l'Italie, de l'Amérique et de l'Asie, dont les fenêtres et les terrasses à présent pleines d'éclairages, de boissons et de brises riches, sont ouvertes à l'esprit des voyageurs et des nobles – qui permettent, aux heures du jour, à toutes les tarentelles des côtes, – et même aux ritournelles des vallées illustres de l'art, de décorer merveilleusement les façades du Palais. Promontoire.

PROMONTORY

The golden dawn and shivering evening find our brig in the open sea opposite this Villa and its surrounding buildings, a promontory as extensive as Epirus and the Peloponnese[24] or the great island of Japan, or Arabia! Shrines lit up by the return of processions; vast views of modern coastal defences; dunes patterned with burning flowers and bacchanals; great canals of Carthage and the Embankments of a sleazy Venice; limp eruptions of Etnas and crevasses of flowers and glacier water; wash-houses bordered by German poplars; the slopes of strange parks in which the tops of Trees of Japan bend down; the curved fronts of 'Royals' or 'Grands' from Scarborough or Brooklyn; and their railways flank, tunnel, overhang the lay-out of this Hotel, chosen from the history of the most elegant and most colossal buildings of Italy, America and Asia, with windows and terraces, at present full of costly lights, drinks and breezes, open to the spirit of the travellers and the nobility – and they allow, during daylight hours, every tarantella of the coasts, – and even the *ritornelli* of the illustrious valleys of art, to decorate to perfection the façades of the Palace. Promontory.

SCÈNES

L'ancienne Comédie poursuit ses accords et divise ses Idylles;

Des boulevards de tréteaux.

Un long pier en bois d'un bout à l'autre d'un champ rocailleux où la foule barbare évolue sous les arbres dépouillés.

Dans des corridors de gaze noire suivant le pas des promeneurs aux lanternes et aux feuilles.

Des oiseaux des mystères s'abattent sur un ponton de maçonnerie mû par l'archipel couvert des embarcations des spectateurs.

Des scènes lyriques accompagnées de flûte et de tambour s'inclinent dans des réduits ménagés sous les plafonds, autour des salons de clubs modernes ou des salles de l'Orient ancien.

La féerie manœuvre au sommet d'un amphithéâtre couronné par les taillis, – Ou s'agite et module pour les Béotiens, dans l'ombre des futaies mouvantes sur l'arête des cultures.

L'opéra-comique se divise sur une scène à l'arête d'intersection de dix cloisons dressées de la galerie aux feux.

SCENES

The ancient Comedy pursues its agreed conventions and allots its Idylls:

Boulevards of stage boards.

A long wooden pier stretching across a rocky field where the barbarian crowd moves about beneath the bare trees.

In corridors of black gauze following the footsteps of the walkers with their lanterns and their leaves.

Birds from the mystery plays alight on a stone landing-stage set in motion by the archipelago swarming with boatloads of spectators.

Lyrical scenes accompanied by flute and drum slope down into recesses created beneath the ceilings, round the public rooms of modern clubs or the halls of the ancient Orient.

The magic spectacle functions at the top of an amphitheatre crowned with thickets, – Or else sets to and adjusts itself to the taste of the Boeotians,[25] in the shadow of waving clusters of trees on the crest of farmland.

The comic opera is divided on a stage at the line of intersection of ten partitions placed between the gallery and the footlights.

SOIR HISTORIQUE

En quelque soir, par exemple, que se trouve le touriste naïf, retiré de nos horreurs économiques, la main d'un maître anime le clavecin des prés; on joue aux cartes au fond de l'étang, miroir évocateur des reines et des mignonnes, on a les saintes, les voiles, et les fils d'harmonie, et les chromatismes légendaires, sur le couchant.

Il frissonne au passage des chasses et des hordes. La comédie goutte sur les tréteaux de gazon. Et l'embarras des pauvres et des faibles sur ces plans stupides!

A sa vision esclave, – l'Allemagne s'échafaude vers des lunes; les déserts tartares s'éclairent – les révoltes anciennes grouillent dans le centre du Céleste Empire, par les escaliers et les fauteuils de rois – un petit monde blême et plat, Afrique et Occidents, va s'édifier. Puis un ballet de mers et de nuits connues, une chimie sans valeur, et des mélodies impossibles.

La même magie bourgeoise à tous les points où la malle nous déposera! Le plus élémentaire physicien sent qu'il n'est plus possible de se soumettre à cette atmosphère personnelle, brume de remords physiques, dont la constatation est déjà une affliction.

Non! – Le moment de l'étuve, des mers enlevées, des embrasements souterrains, de la planète emportée, et des exterminations conséquentes, certitudes si peu malignement indiquées dans la Bible et par les Nornes et qu'il sera donné à l'être sérieux de surveiller. – Cependant ce ne sera point un effet de légende!

HISTORIC EVENING

On some evening, let us say, when the innocent tourist finds himself removed from our economic horrors, the hand of a master brings to life the harpsichord of the fields; people are playing cards at the bottom of the pond, a mirror evoking queens and favourites; they have the saintly women, the veils, and the threads of harmony, and the celebrated chromatics, against the sunset.

He shudders as the hunts and the hordes pass by. The play drips on to the grass stage. And the embarrassment of the poor and the weak on these stupid levels!

To his enslaved vision, – Germany scaffolds upward to moons; the Tartar deserts light up – ancient revolts rumble at the heart of the Celestial Empire, on the stairways and in the armchairs of kings – a little world, pale and flat, Africa and Occidents, is going to be built. Next a ballet of known oceans and nights, a valueless chemistry, and impossible melodies.

The same bourgeois magic wherever the mail boat sets us down! The most elementary physicist can feel that it is no longer possible to submit oneself to this private atmosphere, this fog of physical remorse, whose very existence is already an affliction.

No! – The day of the furnace, of seas swept away, of underground conflagrations, of the planet carried off, and the resulting exterminations, certainties so tamely indicated by the Bible and the Norns[26] which it will fall to the serious person to examine. – But there will be nothing legendary about it!

BOTTOM

La réalité étant trop épineuse pour mon grand caractère, – je me trouvai néanmoins chez ma dame, en gros oiseau gris bleu s'essorant vers les moulures du plafond et traînant l'aile dans les ombres de la soirée.

Je fus, au pied du baldaquin supportant ses bijoux adorés et ses chefs-d'œuvre physiques, un gros ours aux gencives violettes et au poil chenu de chagrin, les yeux aux cristaux et aux argents des consoles.

Tout se fit ombre et aquarium ardent. Au matin, – aube de juin batailleuse, – je courus aux champs, âne, claironnant et brandissant mon grief, jusqu'à ce que les Sabines de la banlieue vinrent se jeter à mon poitrail.

BOTTOM

Reality being too tricky for my lofty nature, – I was nonetheless there at my lady's, in the form of a big blue-grey bird soaring towards the mouldings on the ceiling and dragging my wings in the shadows of the evening.

At the foot of the canopy supporting her adored jewels and her physical masterpieces, I became a big bear with violet gums and fur grizzled with grief, my eyes on the crystal and the silverware on the console tables.

Everything became dark and burning aquarium. In the morning, – a bellicose June dawn, – I ran to the fields, an ass, trumpeting and brandishing my grievance, until the Sabine women[27] from the suburbs came and threw themselves on my breast.

H

Toutes les monstruosités violent les gestes atroces d'Hortense.
Sa solitude est la mécanique érotique, sa lassitude, la dynamique
amoureuse. Sous la surveillance d'une enfance elle a été, à des
époques nombreuses, l'ardente hygiène des races. Sa porte est
ouverte à la misère. Là, la moralité des êtres actuels se décorpore
en sa passion ou en son action – Ô terrible frisson des amours
novices sur le sol sanglant et par l'hydrogène clarteux! trouvez
Hortense.

H

All things unnatural violate the atrocious gestures of Hortense. Her solitude is erotic mechanics, her weariness, the dynamics of love. Under a childhood's supervision she has been, at numerous periods, the passionate hygiene of races. Her door is open to destitution. There, the morality of present beings is disembodied in her passion or her action. O terrible thrill of inexperienced loves on the bloodied ground and in the clearish hydrogen! guess who Hortense is.

MOUVEMENT

Le mouvement de lacet sur la berge des chutes du fleuve,
Le gouffre à l'étambot,
La célérité de la rampe
L'énorme passade du courant,
Mènent par les lumières inouïes
Et la nouveauté chimique
Les voyageurs entourés des trombes du val
Et du strom.

Ce sont les conquérants du monde
Cherchant la fortune chimique personnelle;
Le sport et le comfort voyagent avec eux;
Ils emmènent l'éducation
Des races, des classes et des bêtes, sur ce Vaisseau.
Repos et vertige
A la lumière diluvienne,
Aux terribles soirs d'étude.

Car de la causerie parmi les appareils, – le sang, les
    fleurs, le feu, les bijoux, –
Des comptes agités à ce bord fuyard,
– On voit, roulant comme une digue au-delà de la route
    hydraulique motrice,
Monstrueux, s'éclairant sans fin, – leur stock d'études; –
Eux chassés dans l'extase harmonique
Et l'héroïsme de la découverte.

Aux accidents atmosphériques les plus surprenants
Un couple de jeunesse s'isole sur l'arche,
– Est-ce ancienne sauvagerie qu'on pardonne? –
Et chante et se poste.

MOVEMENT

The twisting movement against the bank at the river falls,
The chasm at the sternpost,
The swiftness of the ramp,
The vast to-and-fro of the current,
With extraordinary lights
And chemical wonders
Lead the travellers on through the waterspouts of the valley
And the whirlpool.

These are the conquerors of the world
Seeking their private chemical fortunes;
Sport and comfort travel with them;
They carry off the education
Of races, classes and animals, on this Vessel.
Rest and vertigo
In the diluvian light,
During the terrible nights of study.

For from the talk in the midst of machines, – the blood, the
    flowers, the fire, the jewels, –
From the agitated calculations on this fugitive deck,
– You can see, rolling like a dyke beyond the hydraulic
    power of the road,
Monstrous, endlessly alight, – their stock of studies; –
Themselves driven into harmonic ecstasy
And the heroism of discovery.

Amid the most extraordinary atmospheric events
Two young people stand alone on the ark,
– Past savagery excused? –
And sing as they take up their watch.

DÉVOTION

A ma sœur Louise Vanaen de Voringhem: – Sa cornette bleue tournée à la mer du Nord. – Pour les naufragés.

A ma sœur Léonie Aubois d'Ashby. Baou – l'herbe d'été bourdonnante et puante. – Pour la fièvre des mères et des enfants.

A Lulu, – démon – qui a conservé un goût pour les oratoires du temps des Amies et de son éducation incomplète. Pour les hommes! – A Madame ***.

A l'adolescent que je fus. A ce saint vieillard, ermitage ou mission.

A l'esprit des pauvres. Et à un très haut clergé.

Aussi bien à tout culte en telle place de culte mémoriale et parmi tels événements qu'il faille se rendre, suivant les aspirations du moment ou bien notre propre vice sérieux,

Ce soir à Circeto des hautes glaces, grasse comme le poisson, et enluminée comme les dix mois de la nuit rouge, – (son cœur ambre et spunk), – pour ma seule prière muette comme ces régions de nuit et précédant des bravoures plus violentes que ce chaos polaire.

A tout prix et avec tous les airs, même dans des voyages métaphysiques. – Mais plus *alors*.

DEVOTIONS

To my sister Louise Vanaen de Voringhem: – Her blue coif turned towards the North Sea. – For the shipwrecked.

To my sister Léonie Aubois d'Ashby. Baou – the buzzing stink of the summer grass. – For the fever of mothers and children.

To Lulu, – a demon – who has kept her taste for oratories since the days of Girlfriends and her incomplete education. For men! – to Madame ***.

To the adolescent I once was. To that holy old man, hermitage or mission.

To the spirit of the poor. And to a very high-ranking clergy.

Also to all worship in any place of memorial worship and among any events it may be necessary to attend, depending on the aspirations of the moment or indeed our own important vice,

This evening to Circeto[28] of the icy heights, fat as the fish, and illuminated like the ten months of the red night, – (her heart amber and spunk), – as my only prayer silent as these regions of night and preceding exploits more violent than this polar chaos.

At any cost and in any guise, even on metaphysical journeys. – But an end to *and then*.

DÉMOCRATIE

«Le drapeau va au paysage immonde, et notre patois étouffe le tambour.

«Aux centres nous alimenterons la plus cynique prostitution. Nous massacrerons les révoltes logiques.

«Aux pays poivrés et détrempés! – au service des plus monstrueuses exploitations industrielles ou militaires.

«Au revoir ici, n'importe où. Conscrits du bon vouloir, nous aurons la philosophie féroce; ignorants pour la science, roués pour le confort; la crevaison pour le monde qui va. C'est la vraie marche. En avant, route!»

DEMOCRACY

'The flag travels to squalid climes, and our native dialect stifles the throbbing of the drum.

'In the heartland we shall sustain the most cynical prostitution. We shall massacre every justified revolt.

'We're off to the clammy lands of spices! – we serve the most monstrous industrial or military exploitation.

'Good-bye to here, never mind where. We're conscripts of good will, our policies will be ferocious; ignorant of science, we're depraved in our comforts; to hell with the world around us. This is the real march. Forward, let's go!'

GÉNIE

Il est l'affection et le présent puisqu'il a fait la maison ouverte à l'hiver écumeux et à la rumeur de l'été, lui qui a purifié les boissons et les aliments, lui qui est le charme des lieux fuyants et le délice surhumain des stations. Il est l'affection et l'avenir, la force et l'amour que nous, debout dans les rages et les ennuis, nous voyons passer dans le ciel de tempête et les drapeaux d'extase.

Il est l'amour, mesure parfaite et réinventée, raison merveilleuse et imprévue, et l'éternité: machine aimée des qualités fatales. Nous avons tous eu l'épouvante de sa concession et de la nôtre: ô jouissance de notre santé, élan de nos facultés, affection égoïste et passion pour lui, lui qui nous aime pour sa vie infinie . . .

Et nous nous le rappelons et il voyage . . . Et si l'Adoration s'en va, sonne, sa promesse sonne: «Arrière ces superstitions, ces anciens corps, ces ménages et ces âges. C'est cette époque-ci qui a sombré!»

Il ne s'en ira pas, il ne redescendra pas d'un ciel, il n'accomplira pas la rédemption des colères de femmes et des gaîtés des hommes et de tout ce péché: car c'est fait, lui étant, et étant aimé.

Ô ses souffles, ses têtes, ses courses; la terrible célérité de la perfection des formes et de l'action.

Ô fécondité de l'esprit et immensité de l'univers!

Son corps! Le dégagement rêvé, le brisement de la grâce croisée de violence nouvelle!

Sa vue, sa vue! tous les agenouillages anciens et les peines *relevés* à sa suite.

Son jour! l'abolition de toutes souffrances sonores et mouvantes dans la musique plus intense.

Son pas! les migrations plus énormes que les anciennes invasions.

Ô lui et nous! l'orgueil plus bienveillant que les charités perdues.

Ô monde! et le chant clair des malheurs nouveaux!

GENIE

He is affection and the present for making the house open to frothy winter and to the hum of summer; he has purified what we eat and drink and lent magic to fleeting places, superhuman delight to things that stay in place. He is affection and the future, the strength and love that we, standing in rage and weariness, see passing in the stormy sky and in the colours of ecstasy.

He is love, perfectly portioned and reinvented, marvellous and unforeseen reason, he is eternity: beloved machine of all that is inevitable. We have all known the terror of his concessions and of our own: such delight in our health, impetus of our faculties, selfish affection and passion for him, for him who loves us throughout his unending life . . .

And we recall him and he moves off . . . And if Adoration moves away, ringing, his promise rings: 'Away with these superstitions, these former bodies, this coupledom, these ages. They belong to the age that has drowned!'

He will not go away, he will not descend again from some heaven, he will not carry out the redemption of women's anger or men's joys and of all that sin: all that is done, because he exists and he is loved.

His breaths, his heads, his flights; the terrible swiftness with which forms and action are perfected!

What richness of the mind and immensity of the universe!

His body! the release we've dreamed of, the splintering of grace crossed with a new form of violence!

To see him, to see him! all the old knee-bending sorrows *lifted* as he passes.

The light of his day! the abolition of all audible and restless suffering in music more intense.

His footsteps! migrations more enormous than the ancient invasions.

We and him together! pride more benevolent than those wasted charities.

The world! and the clear song of new misfortunes!

Il nous a connus tous et nous a tous aimés. Sachons, cette
nuit d'hiver, de cap en cap, du pôle tumultueux au château, de
la foule à la plage, de regards en regards, forces et sentiments
las, le héler et le voir, et le renvoyer, et sous les marées et au
haut des déserts de neige, suivre ses vues, ses souffles, son corps,
son jour.

He has known us all, loved us all. Let us learn, this winter's night, from cape to cape, from the tumultuous pole to the castle, from the crowd to the coast, from glance to glance, our strength and our feelings wearied, to hail him and see him, and to dismiss him, and, beneath the tides and high in the deserts of snow, to follow his vision, his breathing, his body, his light.

NOTES TO
Illuminations

¹ Eucharis: a nymph, companion to Calypso in Fénelon's utopian work *Télémaque* (1699). The Greek name means 'full of grace'.

² Cherubino: the character from Beaumarchais's *Marriage of Figaro*, young, naive, charming and desperate to be in love. The role, as embodied in Mozart's *Le nozze di Figaro*, is associated with cross-dressing.

³ Molochs: Moloch was a cruel god of the Ammonites to whom children were sacrificed.

⁴ Assassins: the word is derived from the Arabic *hashshashin* (hashish-eaters). The Hashshashin were a sect of dedicated murderers, devoted to their leader and inspired by the drug, which was said to procure a vision of paradise.

⁵ Erinnyes: vengeful Furies who notably pursued Orestes. Their pacification by Athene transforms them into the Eumenides (Kindly Ones) and is closely implicated with the foundation of Athens and thereby of democracy. See Aeschylus' *Oresteia*. Rimbaud clearly rejects this idea of pacification here.

⁶ Nebuchadnezzar: king of Babylon, a city famous for its palaces and hanging gardens, but, more importantly here, a city of tyranny, luxury and corruption. The view of Paris and London particularly as 'modern Babylons' was a frequent topic of nineteenth-century literature.

⁷ The word is hard to decipher in the manuscript. Rather than leave a blank I have hazarded a reading congruent with the other Indian allusions (rupees, nabob) in the text.

⁸ Sainte-Chapelle: the famous gothic edifice in Paris.

⁹ Alleghanys: American mountain range.

¹⁰ Rolands: Roland is the best-known of the heroes of medieval French epic.

¹¹ Mabs: Mab is a fairy figure, the midwife of the fairies, whom they employed to deliver man's brain of dreams. See Shakespeare, *Romeo and Juliet*, I, iv.

¹² 'the deer suckle ... Diana': this reverses the idea of Diana as goddess of the hunt and suggests a return to a golden age.

¹³ Bacchantes: votaries of Bacchus, god of wine.

¹⁴ *wasserfall*: the German for waterfall has been retained as in Rimbaud's text.

[15] Sodoms: Sodom is one of the cities destroyed by God (see Genesis xviii, xix); figuratively, it is any centre of vice and depravity.

[16] Solyma: old name for Jerusalem.

[17] Meander: classical name of a river with a winding course in Asia Minor.

[18] Boucher: French painter (1703–70) of pastoral and mythological scenes.

[19] Ossian: legendary Gaelic bard. Often depicted in paintings as singing against a wild seascape.

[20] Samaria: Old Testament city notorious for the corruption of its inhabitants.

[21] The Guarinis are South American Indians.

[22] Psyche: lost her lover Eros when she ignored his warning that they should make love in the dark without her ever seeing him. After many trials she rejoined him and was immortalized.

[23] St Anthony's visions, sent by the devil to tempt him.

[24] Epirus, Peloponnese: provinces of Ancient Greece.

[25] Boeotians: a people of Ancient Greece considered to be rude, dull and unlettered by the Athenians; hence any dull-witted person.

[26] Norns: the Fates in Norse mythology.

[27] The Sabine women were abducted by the Romans when they were short of wives.

[28] Circeto: [?] an amalgam of Circe, the enchantress of the *Odyssey* who turned men into swine, and Ceto, the sea-monster aspect of Eurybia, ruler of the sea. This is highly speculative and, like the other names in this litany-poem, this one is likely to be a private invention.

SOME RESPONSES TO RIMBAUD

W. H. Auden, *Collected Shorter Poems 1927–1957* (London: Faber & Faber, 1966), p. 126

RIMBAUD

The nights, the railway-arches, the bad sky,
His horrible companions did not know it;
But in that child the rhetorician's lie
Burst like a pipe: the cold had made a poet.

Drinks bought him by his weak and lyric friend
His five wits systematically deranged,
To all accustomed nonsense put an end;
Till he from lyre and weakness was estranged.

Verse was a special illness of the ear;
Integrity was not enough; that seemed
The hell of childhood: he must try again.

Now, galloping through Africa, he dreamed
Of a new self, a son, an engineer,
His truth acceptable to lying men.

John Pilling, 'Arthur Rimbaud', in *An Introduction to Fifty Modern European Poets* (London: Pan, 1982), pp. 47–55

Rimbaud, preparatory to abandoning literature altogether, abandoned verse in favour of the prose poem; there are arguably no finer examples of the genre in French literature than the 'stories' (as Rimbaud called them) of *A Season in Hell* and . . . *Illuminations*. The prose poem evidently gave Rimbaud a special purchase on the 'something new' that his letter to Paul Demeny was so insistent about . . . The end of Rimbaud's poetic career is a lot less clear than its beginnings, which is one reason why

the mystique which has grown up around his name is in no danger of diminishing. It is not known, and presumably now never will be, whether Rimbaud abandoned literature in despite of having 'reinvented' love or in despair of doing so. Even in default of any definitive solution to the problems that his meteoric career throws up, it seems certain that Rimbaud will continue to be the cardinal modern example of the two polarities available to poets of a kindred disposition: to transform the world and to keep silent.

Norbert Bonenkamp, 'Exit and save', in *A New History of French Literature*, ed. Denis Hollier (Cambridge, Mass., and London: Harvard University Press, 1989), pp. 758–61

Nothing ... became Rimbaud's literary career like the leaving of it. It is hard not to be seduced by the image of a meteoric adolescent poet burning himself out in rage against the constraints of Western culture ... The combination of Rimbaud's precociousness, his abandonment of literature, the dearth of facts about his life ... and the difficulty and intensity of his texts has given rise to a body of contradictory myths, summarised by René Etiemble: Rimbaud the symbolist, the vagrant, the surrealist, the Bolshevik, the bourgeois, the crook, the pervert, the prophet, the superman, the Christian, and more. But the most paradoxically attractive aspect of the myth for literary history remains the fact that, as Stéphane Mallarmé put it, 'he amputated himself, alive, from poetry' ...

In reality, the chronology of Rimbaud's departure from literature is unclear. Scholars long considered *Une Saison en enfer* to be his last work because it ends with a poem entitled 'Adieu' ... This literary farewell to literature made a good story, but there now exists considerable evidence to suggest that some of the texts collected in *Illuminations* were written after *Une Saison*. And indeed, a close reading of Rimbaud's work indicates that it consists all along in various attempts to escape 'literature' ... In a sense Rimbaud never stopped writing. His Ethiopian correspondence makes up the bulk of his ... complete writing. The challenge to the reader, then, is to learn how to read Rimbaud's escape from literary boundaries *within* his poems and not just *after* them.

Kristin Ross, 'Commune Culture', in *A New History of French Literature*, ed. Hollier, pp. 751–8

In a letter written 17 April 1871, Rimbaud celebrates [the] cacophony of verbal and visual images in the streets as the focus of his experience of Paris: 'Let's talk Paris ... We stopped in front of engravings by A[drien] Marie, *Les Vengeurs* [*The Avengers*], *Les Faucheurs de la mort* [*Death's Reapers*]; and especially caricatures by [Jules] Draner and Faustin [Betheder] ... The items of the day were *Le mot d'ordre* [Henri Rochefort's Commune newspaper] and the admirable fantasies by [Jules] Vallès and [Eugène] Vermersch in *Le cri du peuple* ... Such was literature ... from 25 February to 10 March.' Rimbaud expands the boundaries of literature to include propaganda, political 'fantasies', engravings, and caricatures: ephemeral, satirical genres afloat in a complex set of social discourses and representations. Literature's function, it appears, is to point directly to an entirely revolutionary situation: its affiliation is with the slogan, the call to action (the *mot d'ordre*). More than any other nineteenth-century French poetry, Rimbaud's work, like a forgotten synecdoche of the Commune, has been transmitted to twentieth-century readers mainly in the form of a series of slogans: 'Changer la vie' (Change life); 'L'amour est à réinventer' (Love must be reinvented); 'Il faut être absolument moderne' (We must be absolutely modern).

Michael Riffaterre, 'Sylleptic symbols: Rimbaud's "Mémoire"', in *Nineteenth-Century French Poetry*, ed. Christopher Prendergast (Cambridge: Cambridge University Press, 1990), pp. 178–98

In the case of Rimbaud, deciphering symbols has been ... problematic because the image of the poet has hidden the poetry and warped its interpretation. The substitution of writers for their writing is a widespread fallacy, but it has raised more obstacles between the readers and Rimbaud's work because of his visibility as a man and as a myth. The scandal surrounding his life, at least in the eyes of his contemporaries, and the aura of his precocious genius, have made the temptation irresistible to explain away textual difficulties as autobiographical allu-

sions, when they actually stem from the semiotic make-up of verbal symbols . . .

My aim is to focus on the text's formal features. No interpretation of a poem . . . can ever be specific and reliable unless based on such features. No generalisation towards a definition of Rimbaud's manner can be made without such analyses as its preconditions.

SUGGESTIONS FOR FURTHER READING

The reader is better served in French than in English in this area, but I have tried hard to keep the English reader in mind.

For the reader who wishes to explore Rimbaud's biography there are the following.

Borer, Alain, and Andrée Montègre (eds), *Arthur Rimbaud: Oeuvre–Vie* (Paris: Arléa, 1991)

Eigeldinger, Frédéric, and André Gendre, *Delahaye témoin de Rimbaud* (Neuchâtel: Baconnière, 1974)

Nicholl, Charles, *Somebody Else: Arthur Rimbaud in Africa, 1880–91* (London: Cape, 1997)

Rickword, Edgell, *Rimbaud: The Boy and the Poet* (1924; rev. edn London: Daimon Press, 1963)

Starkie, Enid, *Arthur Rimbaud* (1938; rev. edn London: Hamish Hamilton, 1947)

Steinmetz, Jean-Luc, *Arthur Rimbaud: Une Question de présence* (Paris: Tallandier, 1991)

The following contain either useful commentary on *A Season in Hell* and *Illuminations*, or approaches to Rimbaud that are relevant to these two works.

Ahearn, Edward J., *Rimbaud: Visions and Habitations* (Berkeley and London: University of California Press, 1983)

Cohn, Robert Greer, *The Poetry of Rimbaud* (Princeton, NJ: Princeton University Press, 1973)

Hackett, C. A., *Rimbaud: A Critical Introduction* (Cambridge: Cambridge University Press, 1981)

Little, Roger, *Rimbaud: Illuminations* (London: Grant & Cutler, 1983).

Monroe, Jonathan, *A Poverty of Objects: The Prose Poem and the*

Politics of Genre (Ithaca, NY, and London: Cornell University Press, 1987)

Murphy, Steve, *Le Premier Rimbaud ou L'apprentissage de la subversion* (Lyons and Paris: Presses Universitaires de Lyon/Editions du CNRS, 1990)

Poulet, Georges, *Exploding Poetry*, trans. Françoise Meltzer (Chicago, Ill.: University of Chicago Press, 1984)

Richard, Jean-Pierre, 'Rimbaud ou la poésie du devenir', in *Poésie et profondeur* (Paris: Seuil, 1955)

Rimbaud, Arthur, *Illuminations: Coloured Plates*, ed. Nick Osmond (London: Athlone Press, 1976)

Ross, Kristin, *The Emergence of Social Space: Rimbaud and the Paris Commune* (Minneapolis: University of Minnesota Press, 1989)

Wing, Nathaniel, 'The autobiography of rhetoric: on reading Rimbaud's *Une Saison en enfer*' in *The Limits of Narrative* (Cambridge: Cambridge University Press, 1986)

INDEX OF ENGLISH TITLES

Adieu 51
After the Flood 59
Alchemy of the Word 31
Anguish 121
Bad Blood 5
Barbaric 125
Being Beauteous 72
Bottom 143
Bridges, The 93
Childhood 61
Cities I 99
Cities II 105
City 95
Classical 71
Clearance Sale 127
Dawn 111
Democracy 151
Departure 79
Devotions 149
Fairy 129
First Delirium 23
Flowers 113
Foolish Virgin, The 23
Genie 153
H 145
Historic Evening 141
Hunger 37
Illuminations 57

Impossibility 43
Infernal Bridegroom, The 23
Lightning 47
Lives 75
Metropolitan 123
Morning 49
Morning of Drunken Ecstasy 85
Movement 147
Mystical 109
Night in Hell 17
On Show 69
Phrases 87
Promontory 137
Royalty 81
Ruts 97
Seascape 117
Scenes 139
Season in Hell, A 1
Second Delirium 31
Song of the Highest Tower 35
Tale 67
Tawdry Nocturne 115
To a Reason 83
Tramps 103
Vigils 107
War 135
Winter Festival 119
Workers 91
Youth 131

INDEX OF FRENCH TITLES

Adieu 50
Alchimie du verbe 30
Angoisse 120
Antique 70
Après le Déluge 58
Aube 110
A une raison 82
Barbare 124
Being Beauteous 73
Bottom 142
Chanson de la plus haute
  tour 34
Conte 66
Délires I 22
Délires II 30
Démocratie 150
Départ 78
Dévotion 148
L'Éclair 46
Enfance 60
L'Epoux infernale 22
Faim 36
Fairy 128
Fête d'hiver 118
Fleurs 112
Génie 152
Guerre 134
H 144
Illuminations 57

L'Impossible 42
Jeunesse 130
Marine 116
Matin 48
Matinée d'ivresse 84
Mauvais sang 4
Métropolitain 122
Mouvement 146
Mystique 108
Nocturne vulgaire 114
Nuit de l'enfer 16
Ornières 96
Ouvriers 90
Parade 68
Phrases 86
Pont, Les 92
Promontoire 136
Royauté 80
Saison en Enfer, Une 1
Scènes 138
Soir historique 140
Solde 126
Vagabonds 102
Veillées 106
Vierge folle 22
Vies 74
Ville 94
Villes I 98
Villes II 104

ACKNOWLEDGEMENTS

The translator and publishers wish to thank the following for permission to use copyright material:

Faber and Faber Ltd and Random House, Inc. for W. H. Auden, 'Rimbaud' from *W. H. Auden: Collected Poems*, edited by Edward Mendelson. © 1940, renewed 1968 by W. H. Auden;

Every effort has been made to trace the copyright holders but if any have been inadvertently overlooked the publishers will be pleased to make the necessary arrangement at the first opportunity.